W0372301

Abitur Skript

Englisch

Abi Niedersachsen – 2023

STARK

Bildnachweis:
S. 7: Frau mit Kinderwagen, Frau mit Krückstock © Leremy. Shutterstock
S. 18: Frau mit Krückstock © ankudi. Shutterstock, Mann mit Koffern © RedKoala. Shutterstock, Familie © kazenouta. Shutterstock, Flagge Indien © tamarindarts. 123rf.com, Flagge USA © charnsitr. Shutterstock
S. 42: Hütte, Ähre © firkin – OpenClipart, Hand mit Messer © laobc – OpenClipart
S. 52: Frankenstein © Palau. Shutterstock, Monster © Skeleton Icon. Shutterstock, Schiff © LjubodragG. Shutterstock

Inhalt

Hamlet (eA)

Verfasst von:
Rainer Jacob (Short Stories, *Frankenstein*, *Hamlet*),
Sonja Corleis *(Gran Torino)*, Dr. Bernd Klewitz *(Mother to Mother)*

Vorwort

Liebe Schülerinnen und Schüler,

dieses handliche Skript bietet Ihnen umfassende Informationen zu allen **verbindlichen Materialien** (Pflichtlektüren und -film), die Sie für die **Abiturprüfung 2023** im Fach Englisch kennen müssen.
Dank der knappen, übersichtlichen Darstellung eignet es sich besonders zur Auffrischung und Wiederholung des Prüfungsstoffs kurz vor dem Abitur:

- Anhand der Kennzeichnung im Inhaltsverzeichnis können Sie ersehen, welche Materialien sowohl im **grundlegenden** als auch im **erhöhten Anforderungsniveau** verbindlich sind, welche nur für das erhöhte Niveau vorausgesetzt werden und welche nur an **Beruflichen** bzw. nur an **Allgemeinbildenden Gymnasien** zu behandeln sind.
- Zu jedem Werk finden Sie die wichtigsten **Fakten**, eine **Zusammenfassung der Handlung** und eine Übersicht über die zentralen **Figuren**.
- Unter „Themes and interpretation“ können Sie **Interpretationsansätze** zu den Werken nachlesen, die Ihnen bei der Bearbeitung von möglichen Abituraufgaben helfen können. In der Textaufgabe wird unter Umständen von Ihnen verlangt, inhaltliche Aspekte aus dem Prüfungstext (den Sie im Abitur erstmals zu Gesicht bekommen) zu den verpflichtenden Materialien (die Sie aus dem Unterricht kennen) in Bezug zu setzen. Die in diesem Skript behandelten Themen orientieren sich an den vom Niedersächsischen Kultusministerium festgelegten „verbindlichen Unterrichtsaspekten“ und sind so für die Abiturprüfung besonders relevant (siehe Übersicht auf der folgenden Seite).
- Zahlreiche **Schaubilder** und **Beispiele** helfen Ihnen, sich das Gelernte besser einzuprägen.

Viel Erfolg beim Lernen mit diesem Skript und im Abitur!

Kerncurriculum und verbindliche Materialien

Individual and Society	
identity	***Frankenstein:*** questions of (human) identity
ethnic, cultural and linguistic diversity	***Mother to Mother:*** ethnic and cultural diversity **Five Postcolonial Short Stories:** postcolonial experience, displacement: questions of belonging and identity ***Gran Torino:*** cultural clashes
gender and sexual diversity	
Science and Technology	
chances and risks	***Frankenstein:*** ethics of science, the role of nature
visions of the future	
the media, e. g. the influence of the media on public opinion and personal life	
the digital revolution	
Globalisation	
effects on the world of work	
impact on personal lives	
global responsibility concerning e. g. politics, the environment, economy	
English as a global language	
Beliefs, Values and Norms in Society: Tradition and Change	
Britishness	
the American experience	***Gran Torino:*** cultural clashes, the role of gang culture and violence
postcolonial / neo-colonial experiences	***Mother to Mother:*** ethnic and cultural diversity, apartheid in South Africa, accountability and justice **Five Postcolonial Short Stories:** postcolonial experience, displacement: questions of belonging and identity
migration effects on the world of work	
Shakespeare (nur eA)	
the world that made him	***Hamlet:*** fate vs. free will, the role(s) of women, questions of morality
modern adaptations	

Five Postcolonial Short Stories

1 "Loose Change"

Background information

The National Portrait Gallery London	– collection of portraits of historically important and famous British people – today also portraits of Black British personalities, but these were for a long time marginalised in collective memory of the country – examples that narrator shows to Laylor are all of White people → narrator's view of British history seems to be "White"
2005: unrest in Uzbekistan	– protests against violation of basic human rights – violence against protesters and persecution of journalists and dissidents
Windrush generation	– 1948: HMT Empire Windrush brought the first large group of immigrants from the West Indies and marks the beginning of mass immigration to the UK – narrator's grandmother probably belonged to Windrush generation

1.1 Key facts about the short story

- **author:** Andrea Levy (1956–2019), born in London to Jamaican parents
- **year of publication:** 2005
- **genre:** short story
- **setting:** London (lavatory and café of National Portrait Gallery)
- **narrative perspective:** first-person narration (first-person central: narrator is also the protagonist)
- **content:** The narrator is given a few coins by a young woman, who turns out to be a political refugee. She feels sympathy for the girl, but fails to help her.
- **explanation of title:** few coins as element which connects the two women, symbolises the narrator's feeling of obligation, but also her final desertion of Laylor

1.2 Plot

- the narrator is short of change and receives coins from a young woman (Laylor) in the lavatory of the National Portrait Gallery in London
- judging from her accent, Laylor is obviously a foreigner (narrator conjectures she could be a Spanish tourist)
- while the narrator is in the lavatory, Laylor leaves to look at pictures in the gallery
- the narrator finds her there and together they look at several pictures, their tastes are quite different
- the narrator invites Laylor for a cup of tea to give her back her change
- in the conversation the narrator learns that Laylor is from Tashkent, Uzbekistan
- Laylor's brother comes to the café and they argue in their language
- after he has left, the narrator learns that Laylor and her brother had to flee from Tashkent and are sleeping rough on London's streets
- the narrator begins to observe details about Laylor's scruffy appearance (dirty fingernails, crumpled collar)
- she knows deep down that she has the means to put Laylor and her brother up at least for some time
- she thinks of how warmly her grandmother, who came from the Caribbean and was also sleeping rough, remembered a stranger helping her
- however, putting these considerations and memories aside, the narrator simply leaves on the pretext of fetching tissues for Laylor

1.3 Characters

the narrator

- Londoner, **third-generation immigrant** (grandmother emigrated from the Caribbean to the UK)
- single mother, working at school, **middle-class background** with comfortable three-bedroom house
- describes herself as **typical Londoner:** keeps herself to herself, rather **distanced** to strangers
- rather out of **obligation and responsibility**, gives up her unapproachable manner and becomes more open with Laylor
- however, sees this change in her behaviour (“this fraternisation”) as defeat
- when she realises that the homeless girl is in a desperate situation, **two conflicting interests:** would like to be welcoming and helpful (like a stranger once was towards her **grandmother**), but on the other hand does not want to be involved in Laylor’s poverty
- finally leaves the girl alone in a rather **cowardly** fashion

Laylor

- about 18-year-old **refugee from Uzbekistan**, daughter of politically prosecuted parents
- black hair, wide black eyes, round face, a solid jaw line, speaks with an accent
- partly **unrefined manners** (in the narrator’s view): speaks with a loud voice in public, drinks tea despite specks of dust in it, “forces” her story on stranger
- however, **disarming openness:** only person to help the narrator out with coins (despite her poverty), partly innocent good mood and interest in arts (despite her forlorn situation)
- **desperate and helpless:** homeless, scruffy outer appearance, fears for her parents

the narrator's grandmother

- does not appear in the story in person, but **important influence** on narrator
- came to the UK as an **immigrant from the Caribbean**
- looking back, she **keeps praising her "Good Samaritan"** who put her up when she first arrived
- today, however, she passionately **opposes immigration**, denouncing refugees and asylum seekers as scroungers and troublemakers
- both her memories of being a helpless immigrant and her current hostility and xenophobia seem to influence the narrator's attitude

Plotline in **"Loose Change"**

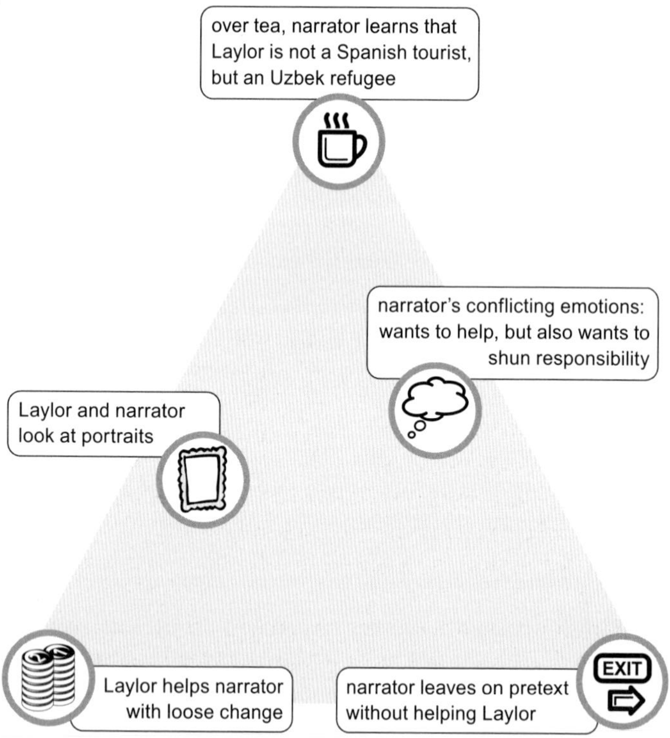

2 "She Shall Not Be Moved"

2.1 Key facts about the short story

- **author:** Shereen Pandit (born in Cape Town), went into exile in the UK in 1987
- **year of publication:** 2005
- **genre:** short story
- **setting:** London (on the bus)
- **narrative perspective:** first-person narration (first-person central: narrator is also the protagonist)
- **content:** the narrator, a political refugee to Britain, fails to live up to her principles, because she does not stand up against racists hindering a Somali woman from parking her pram in the pram space on the bus
- **explanation of title:** Somali woman refuses to be moved and takes offences with dignity; based on spiritual "I Shall Not Be Moved" that became a protest song among Civil Rights activists

2.2 Plot

- the narrator boards a crowded bus with her daughter Mariam
- the aisle is blocked by a Somali woman with a toddler and a pram
- the bus driver shouts at her to move down the aisle, but she cannot
- two White women are occupying the fold-up seats where the pram should be parked and refuse to give up their seats despite there being free seats elsewhere on the bus
- instead of telling off the White women, the bus driver yells at the Somali woman to fold up the pram or leave the bus
- the narrator is shocked by the driver's behaviour but does not say anything
- the Somali woman remains standing proudly despite the driver's attack, the White women's racist remarks and the narrator's attempt to offer her seat to her

- when an elderly White lady enters the bus, the narrator does not want to give up her seat for her despite her usual manners ("reverse racis[m]")
- Mariam cannot understand why her mother neither helps the Somali woman nor lets her give up her seat for the elderly White lady
- when the Somali woman leaves the bus and the narrator advises her to report the driver, she says it is no good and calls him a slave
- to make up for being a bad role model for Mariam and betraying her values, the narrator takes her daughter out for an extra treat, but cannot stop thinking about her failure to speak out

2.3 Characters

narrator

- **Black woman**, who came to the UK because of her fight for political rights
- **strong convictions about right and wrong**, which she also attempts to teach to her daughter
- however, when she **witnesses racism** on the bus, she does not interfere and offers **numerous excuses for not getting involved**
- still, she regrets keeping quiet and feels ashamed that she has **betrayed her own principles**

Mariam

- the narrator's daughter
- rather delicate little girl
- has been brought up to be **respectful** and **outspoken** when she witnesses wrongdoing
- tries to urge the narrator to speak up against the White women's racist behaviour → **disappointed and confused** when she sees her mother's "wrong" behaviour (not offering a seat to elderly lady, not coming to the aid of woman in trouble)

Somali woman

- woman with two small children
- wearing traditional clothing
- **strong** and **proud** character, puts up with insults and discrimination with dignity
- calls the bus driver "a slave" and stresses that she is **not a slave**

two White women

- narrator calls them "Cardie" and "Mac" (because one of them is wearing a cardigan, the other a colourless stained Mac)
- both in their 50s
- look rather poor, rough and uneducated to the narrator
- **prejudiced against Black people:** racist remarks and comments, deliberately refuse to move seats (to teach "who is boss here")

bus driver

- despite being **Black** himself, **aggressive towards Somali woman**
- turns a blind eye to the White ladies' behaviour, does not stand up for the Somali woman
- **seems to have accepted racism** and is apparently afraid of getting into conflict with racist women himself

Who's Who in **"She Shall Not Be Moved"**

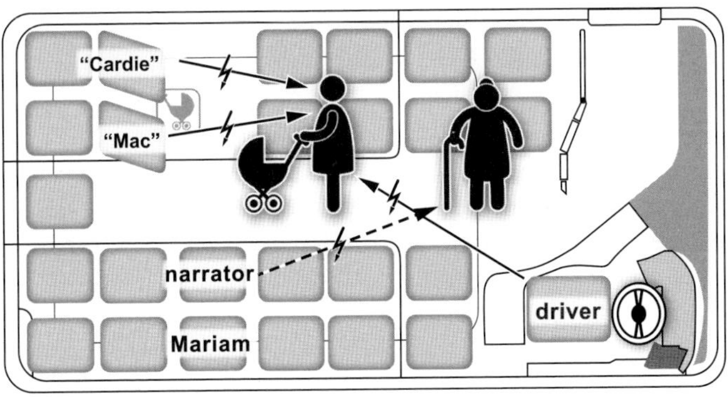

3 "The Escape"

Background information

Eid ul Fitr	– "Festival of Breaking the Fast" – religious festive day celebrated by Muslims to mark the end of Ramadan
Lahore	– second-largest city in Pakistan – capital of Punjab province
Data Darbar	– shrine in Lahore – considered to be the most sacred place in the city
Enoch Powell (1912–1998)	– Conservative British politician – held a notorious speech against immigration in 1968
Uganda under Idi Amin	– In the 1970s, Asians who had successfully settled in Uganda were forced to leave the country by dictator Idi Amin. – Many sought refuge in the UK afterwards.

3.1 Key facts about the short story

- **author:** Qaisra Shahraz (*1958), born in Pakistan, has lived in Manchester since the age of 9
- **year of publication:** 2009
- **genre:** short story
- **setting:** England (Manchester area) – Pakistan (Lahore)
- **narrative perspective:** third-person narration (Samir's viewpoint)
- **content:** 73-year-old Samir, a Pakistani immigrant, who arrived in the UK in the 1960s, visits Pakistan, his land of origin, and realises that his real home is now England
- **explanation of title:** Samir makes several "escapes", the last two are his trip to Pakistan and from there back again to England

3.2 Plot

- Samir, 73-year-old widower, Pakistani immigrant, tells his family he will visit his homeland Pakistan for a few months
- three days later in Pakistan, he is put up by his brother's family and amicably welcomed
- he visits his parents' graves and muses about his wife's recent death as well as his own burial, which he is sure will take place in Manchester
- flashback: Samir remembers the days of his arrival in England where he stayed and worked in various places until he finally settled in Manchester and established a successful knitwear manufacturing business
- Samir calls at the home of a widow his wife supported and promises to continue sponsorship and pay for the education of the widow's daughters
- he leaves to visit the Data Darbar in Lahore and prays for his wife's soul as well as for himself
- Samir returns to his brother's and informs the family (to their surprise) that he will be flying back to England
- on the plane he meets Ibrahim, a man of his age, and both wonder whether their homeland is Pakistan or England
- Samir asks Ibrahim to join him in his new home (an old people's home)
- he leaves his house to his children, instructs them to continue the support of the widow in Pakistan and moves into an old people's home
- Samir feels his escapes are over and he has finally arrived (he calls himself and Ibrahim "the new English babus")

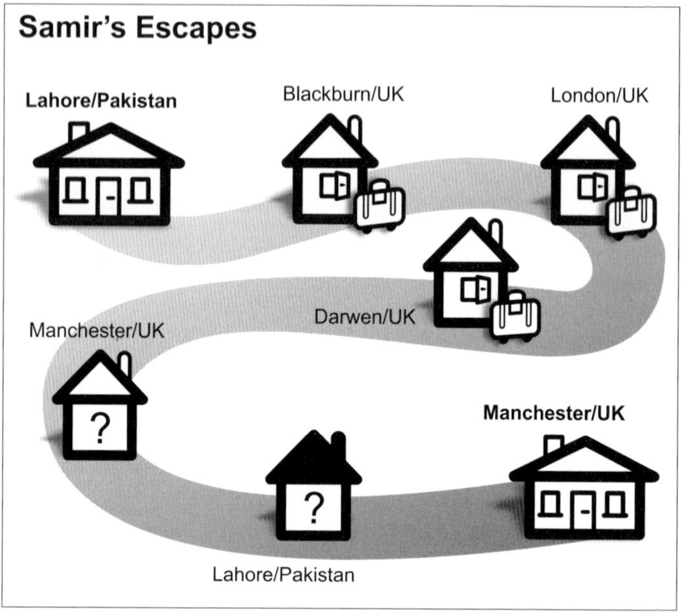

3.3 Characters

Samir

- 73 years old
- born and raised in **Pakistan**, immigrated to the UK in the 1960s, based in **Manchester** area
- **religious** Muslim, **devoted family man**, loves his children and grandchildren
- has made it **from shy, insecure man**, who moved from place to place and job to job, **to successful business and house owner**
- feels **lost since his wife's recent death**
- fuelled by his loneliness, he searches for his **homeland** (and comes to the conclusion that it is now England)

Samir's Manchester family

- Samir has **four children:** two sons and two daughters as well as **several grandchildren**
- all seem financially secure and well-integrated
- treat Samir with **kindness** and **respect**, want to make him feel comfortable
- cherish **Pakistani traditions**, but feel that **England** is **their home** → cannot believe that Samir wants to go back to Pakistan

Samir's Lahore family

- receive Samir very **hospitably**
- still Samir feels like a burden and not really at home there
- **surprised** when Samir calls England his home

4 "The Rain Missed My Face and Fell Straight to My Shoes"

4.1 Key facts about the short story

- **author:** Saeed Taji Farouky, born in London to Palestinian-Egyptian parents, grew up between London and several Middle Eastern cities
- **year of publication:** 2005
- **genre:** short story
- **setting:** London
- **narrative perspective:** first-person narration (first-person central: narrator is also the protagonist)
- **content:** displaced persons work illegally in London; the narrator is at a crossroads: he can either go to Paris with his friends or remain in London alone
- **explanation of title:** symbolises the lack of protection and the difficult living conditions of undocumented immigrants, also small note of hope

4.2 Plot

- Samir, the narrator, sneaks into the cinema where he used to work thanks to the help of his friend Faris and meets his friends Youssef and Hamza there
- Samir tells Youssef that his mother fell ill in Cairo and his family wanted to fly her to London to be treated in the NHS
- to pay for his mother's ticket, Samir stole money from the cinema, was found out and lost his job
- mother was treated in London hospital, but died after 17 days
- Samir now needs money for his mother to be buried in Cairo
- Samir meets Youssef and his friend Aqil, who is from Iraq, in a café
- they criticise the British involvement in the Iraq War and the ensuing chaos (vandalism, destruction of cultural monuments)

- Aqil cannot help Samir ("If I knew where to get money, I would get it!")
- while Samir is working in the kitchen of Café Tangier, Aqil offers him to go to Paris with him and Youssef
- Samir hesitates: he is afraid of being left alone in London and afraid of going with his friends to unknown Paris
- open end: Samir does not know what to do

4.3 Characters

Samir

- **Egyptian**, **undocumented immigrant** in London, always **anxious**, **worried**, afraid of being arrested because he has no papers
- no fixed home, no girlfriend, no steady job
- **drinks** and **smokes** hashish
- **influenced by his friends**, because he is a **rather hesitant** character himself
- not sure about the direction he wants to give to his life
- **does not want to be a criminal** but has to do all kinds of jobs, even illegal ones, just to survive
- **ashamed** of the low jobs he is doing, does not want his family to know, even wishes he were on the run from political persecution to give a sense to his existence, poverty and criminality

Youssef

- **Egyptian**
- **self-assured**, not afraid of people, **strong personality**
- **strong influence** on insecure Samir
- his decision to go to Paris with Aqil seems to be decisive for Samir's future (without Youssef, Samir would feel all alone)

Aqil

- **Iraqi**
- short, stocky, wears thick glasses, former weightlifter

- doctorate degree in physics, left Iraqi army and escaped to England
- works in video shop, **politically interested**, follows the news
- against European and American involvement in Iraq, strong emotional reaction to destruction of cultural items
- sees the downfall of Iraq as a result of the inactivity of his compatriots to fight against European and American influence

Hamza

- Somali
- can speak neither English nor Arabic well
- does not like Samir coming to the cinema, worried about losing his cleaning job

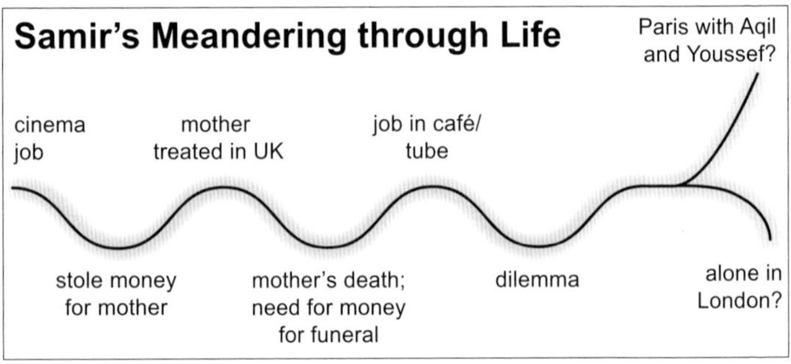

5 "The Third and Final Continent"

5.1 Key facts about the short story

- **author:** Jhumpa Lahiri (*1967), born in London to Bengali Indian parents; family moved to USA when she was three
- **year of publication:** 1999
- **genre:** short story
- **setting:** mainly Boston/USA, also London/UK, Calcutta/India
- **narrative perspective:** first-person narration (first-person central: narrator is also the protagonist)
- **time:** mainly 1960s (1964: India → UK, 1969: UK → USA); 1990s (end of story)
- **content:** the narrator, an immigrant from Calcutta/India, overcomes his loneliness and alienation with the help of his 103-year-old landlady and makes his way up in American society
- **explanation of title:** after living in South Asia (India) and Europe (England), the narrator finally finds his place in America (USA) – the third and final continent of his journey

5.2 Plot

- 1964: narrator leaves India (Bengal) with a certificate in commerce on board an Italian ship bound for England
- in London he lives in a house crowded with penniless Bengali single young men, attends lectures at the London School of Economics and works at university library
- 1969: he flies back to Calcutta to attend his wedding arranged by his older brother and meets his future wife Mala for the first time
- accepts a full-time job in America at library of MIT in Boston
- at first lives in a very basic and noisy room at the YMCA
- moves to a room in the house of an eccentric 103-year-old lady, Mrs. Croft
- he stays there for six weeks and both get on very well together
- leaves Mrs. Croft when Mala arrives

- at first, distant relationship between the newly-wed couple
- when he shows Mala the house where he used to live for six weeks and they meet old Mrs. Croft, who expresses her admiration for Mala, the relationship between the narrator and Mala becomes more intimate
- later, he learns that Mrs. Croft has died and deeply mourns her death
- about 30 years later, the narrator still lives in Boston area, he and his wife are American citizens and their son attends Harvard University

5.3 Characters

narrator

- in his **thirties** in the 1960s (*~1933)
- **educated** and **ambitious**
- lives in **modest circumstances** both in London and Boston, but does not complain (e. g. about frugal meal of cornflakes and milk)
- finds it hard to adapt to America at first and is quite **lonely**
- **polite** and **kind** to Mrs. Croft, admires her for her old age and finally grows quite attached to her
- dutifully complies with the **traditions of his home country** (arranged marriage, cremation ceremony)
- at first **rather disturbed by his wife's presence** and his responsibilities towards her
- however, treats Mala with **understanding** and **respect** and they grow very close and end up having a **loving marriage**

Mrs. Croft

- tiny **103-year-old widow**, almost fierce-looking, speaks in a loud, commanding voice
- raised her children by giving piano lessons after the death of her husband
- quite **fit for her age**, although **not fully mobile** and tends to be **forgetful**

- **independent-minded** although she cannot really care for herself (needs to eat pre-opened soups, for example)
- has her **fixed routine** (always wears the same dress, always sits in the same place, eats the same food)
- **patriotic** (proud of American moon landing)
- **eccentric** (rents only to students from MIT or Harvard, insists on the narrator using the word "splendid")
- **old-fashioned** ideas about decency
- **values narrator's manners and consideration** (handing her the rent money instead of simply depositing it on piano), grows attached to him and also approves of Mala

Mala

- daughter of a schoolteacher, a **good housekeeper** and **well-educated**
- 27 years old at time of **arranged marriage**, not very pretty, has been rejected by several men
- at first very **unhappy and lonely** in her marriage to a stranger and a foreign country (clings to traditional clothing, food, etc.)
- narrator discovers her **kind side** during visit to Mrs. Croft
- they grow very close and both adapt to **America as their new home**
- misses her son when he has moved out

Helen

- Mrs. Croft's daughter, 68 years old, short, thick-waisted, silver hair, pink lipstick
- looks after her elderly mother regularly
- down-to-earth, pragmatic, not overtly emotional about her mother (narrator seems to be more concerned about Mrs. Croft's well-being than her daughter)

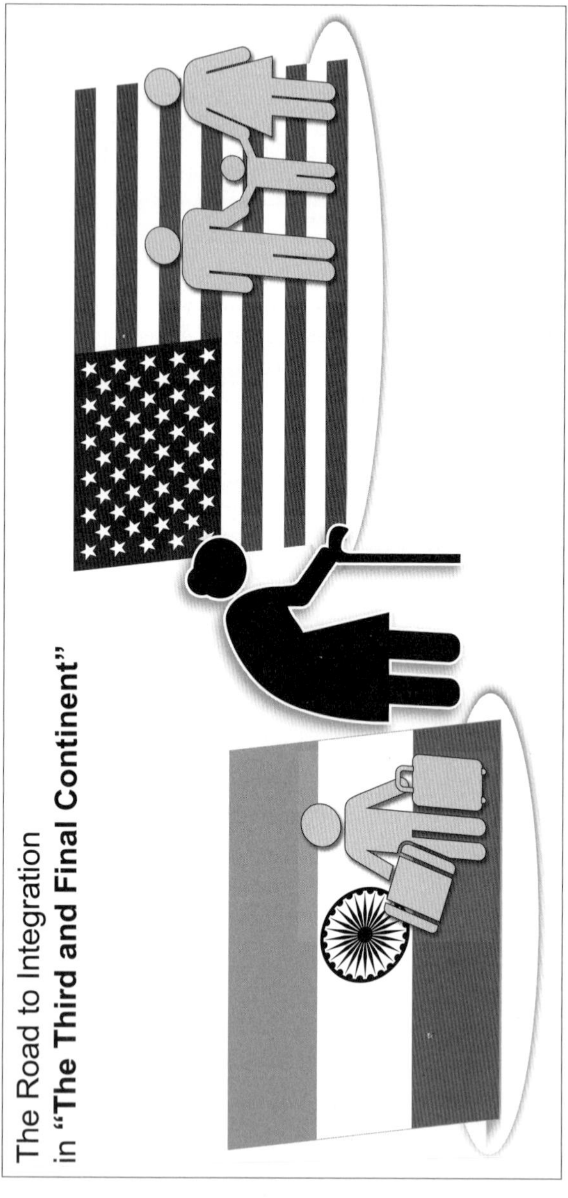
The Road to Integration
in "The Third and Final Continent"

6 Themes and interpretation

The themes dealt with in the short stories relate to the major topics "postcolonial experience" and "displacement: questions of belonging and identity".

Postcolonial experience

Postcolonialism refers, among other things, to the study of how **colonialism** continues to shape the world even after the British Empire or other colonial ventures ended. Both people from formerly **colonised** lands as well as the **colonisers** can still feel the impact of earlier **power relations**.

Displacement: questions of belonging and identity

Displaced persons are people who are forced to **leave their homeland**, usually for reasons that endanger their lives or well-being. Their arrival in a foreign country where they are often met with suspicion, **prejudice** and rejection can result in profound **crises of identity and belonging**. Issues of identity and belonging can also impact **later generations of immigrants** who might feel torn between several cultures.

"Loose Change"

- narrator influenced by **two different sets of values:** her grandmother's own experience of being dependent on a stranger's help and her self-assessment of being a "true Londoner", who keeps out of and aloof from others' trouble
- grandmother's own development from dependent immigrant to UK citizen, who is indignant and prejudiced towards refugees
- Laylor and her brother: because of their sudden hasty flight from Uzbekistan **life has changed completely within a week**
- as soon as Laylor's true status as **homeless and poor refugee** is revealed, met with **suspicion and rejection**
- Laylor and her brother do not seem to know where they could turn to for help

"She Shall Not Be Moved"

- example of **racism** against Somali woman: **ignored** by White passengers, **tacitly accepted** by narrator, even **corroborated** by bus driver
- narrator's feeling that she should **solidarise** with Somali woman, but afraid to endanger her own and possibly her daughter's **safety and comfort**
- **pride** of Somali woman **vs. cowardice and insecurity** of both narrator and bus driver ("slaves")
- narrator has been raised to "show them we're better", i. e. with strong moral principles
- however, Mariam witnesses her mother's weakness and **might internalise seeming inferiority** in the long run
- narrator behaves, in her own words, like a "**reverse racist**", which shows her bitterness and the entrenched mutual distrust

"The Escape"

- Samir as a typical example of feeling **torn between two homes** (wants to escape loneliness in England, but realises that Lahore is no longer his home either)
- **inner loneliness connected to homelessness** though this might not be the real problem
- Samir **has made it in England** and has always believed in the country
- his children represent **second generation of immigrants: cultural ties to Pakistan** (partly even more pronounced than in Samir's generation, e. g. beards to show their heritage), but completely **at home in England**

"The Rain Missed My Face and Fell Straight to My Shoes"

- Samir and his mates are **immigrants without proper documentation**, living in **constant fear of being detected and deported**
- due to their illegal status, **victims of exploitation**, working only in low-skilled, low-wage jobs (nightshift in the Underground, kitchen help, toilet cleaner)
- cannot lead normal lives (Samir: "All I want is to live simply.")

- desperate situation forces them to **break the law** (Aqil: "I left my country to escape from criminals and I came here, and I became a criminal.")
- **dilemma:** Samir's mother has a better chance for medical care in the UK, but emotional connections to homeland (burial in Egypt)
- Samir is **ashamed** to tell his family in Egypt about his demeaning existence
- life without any purpose makes Samir **depressed** (even wishes to be politically persecuted)
- **fears of complete solitude** without his friends, who want to leave London for Paris

"The Third and Final Continent"

- narrator goes through **several stages of alienation and privation** (UK, USA)
- overarching theme of **loneliness** (new country, marriage to a stranger)
- Mrs. Croft, who is quite lonely herself, helps narrator to overcome these feelings
- move to USA **especially difficult for Mala:** speaks only little English, only moves there to follow a husband she hardly knows, loneliness and homesickness
- 30 years later: narrator and Mala's **integration** has been **successful: mix of cultures:** American citizenship, keeping in touch with their Bengali roots
- narrator encourages his son to follow in his footsteps of overcoming challenges, but muses that the **next generation** might even go one step further and give up Bengali traditions

Gran Torino

1 Key facts about the film

- **screenplay:** written by Nick Schenk
- **director and producer:** Clint Eastwood (also stars as main character)
- **release date:** 2008/2009
- **genre: modern-day Western** (plot centring on "lone Cowboy"/hero Walt who takes the law into his own hands), **action movie** (scenes of violence and fighting), **psychological drama** (focus on psychological conflicts, fraught relationships, heartbreaking ending)
- **running time:** ca. 112 minutes
- **structure:** frame of two funerals (Dorothy and Walt Kowalski), development of Walt and Thao's friendship, escalation of gang violence, Thao's process of growing up
- **setting:** Detroit area, Michigan
- **content:** Thao, a young, insecure Hmong teenager, is supposed to steal his elderly neighbour Walt Kowalski's Gran Torino as an initiation rite into gang life. Walt is a recently widowed, embittered and racist Korean War veteran. In the aftermath of the thwarted stealing attempt, Walt develops a close relationship to Thao and his family. Their friendship gives Thao a direction and Walt's life a new meaning, which culminates in his self-sacrifice to free Thao and his sister from the threats of gang violence.

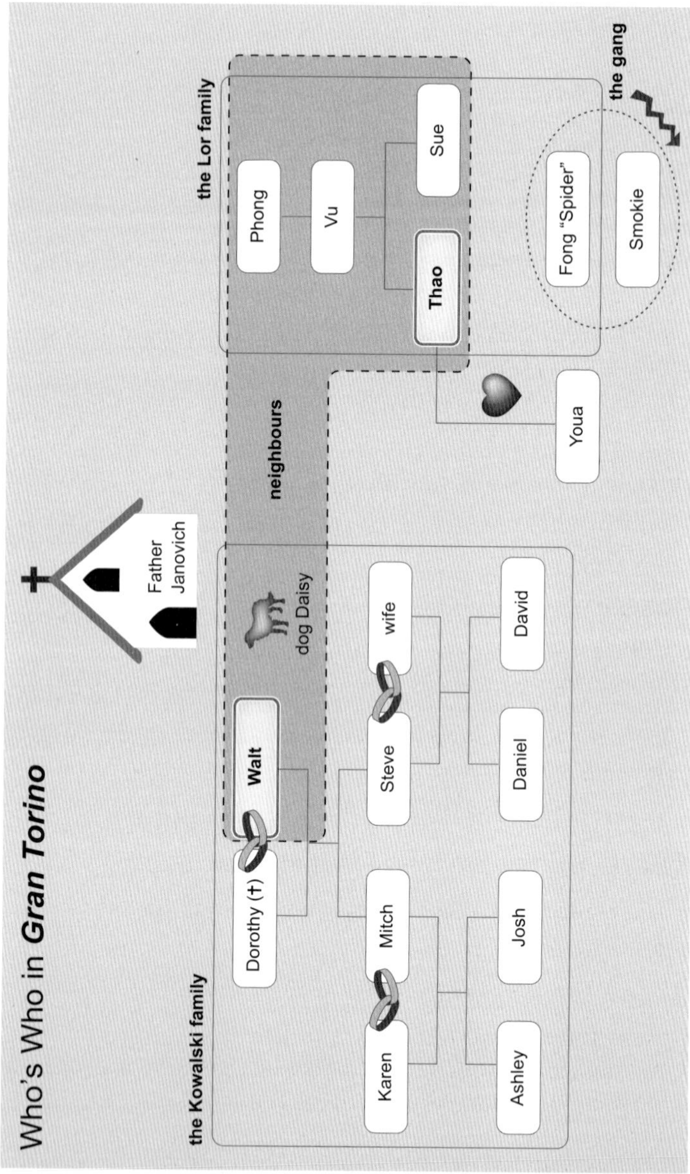
Who's Who in *Gran Torino*
Father Janovich
the Kowalski family
Dorothy (†)
Walt
dog Daisy
Karen
Mitch
Steve
wife
Ashley
Josh
Daniel
David
neighbours
the Lor family
Phong
Vu
Thao
Sue
Youa
Fong "Spider"
Smokie
the gang

2 Plot

Setting 1 | **At the church (ca. 00:45–03:43)**[1]

- Dorothy Kowalski's funeral service
- widower Walt is visibly upset about family's behaviour and Father Janovich's shallow sermon

Setting 2 | **In Walt's house/Outside Walt's house (ca. 03:44–09:44)**

- Walt's grandsons find memorabilia of Korean War in Walt's cellar
- Walt's granddaughter Ashley bluntly asks him to inherit 1972 Gran Torino Sport
- traditional Hmong birth ceremony at Walt's neighbours' house
- Father Janovich wants Walt to go to confession, Walt rejects this

Setting 3 | **Inside the Lors' house (ca. 09:45–11:05)**

- Thao's grandmother Phong complains about Thao not being "the man of the house"

Setting 4 | **On the porches (ca. 11:06–12:40)**

- Walt and Phong suspiciously eye each other from their porches
- Walt refuses Father Janovich's offer for confession again

Setting 5 | **In the street (ca. 12:41–15:08)**

- Hispanic gang bullies Thao
- cousin Spider and his gang help Thao, want him to join them

Setting 6 | **In the Lors' garden (ca. 15:09–17:22)**

- gang pressures Thao into joining them and stealing Walt's Gran Torino

Setting 7 | **At a bar (ca. 17:23–20:04)**

- Father Janovich's next attempt to talk to Walt
- Walt mentions experiences on the Korean battlefield, implying that he knows more about death than the young priest

1 Times refer to the DVD version of *Gran Torino* and may vary slightly when played on different devices.

Setting 8 — **In Walt's house and garage (ca. 20:05–21:17)**

- Thao's attempt to steal the Gran Torino thwarted by Walt pointing a gun at him

Setting 9 — **In Walt's garage and house (ca. 21:18–22:27)**

- telephone call by Walt's son Mitch, only interested in football tickets

Setting 10 — **On Walt's lawn and in the street (ca. 22:28–25:39)**

- Hmong gang harasses Thao
- Walt drives them away by threatening them with rifle

Setting 11 — **On Walt's porch (ca. 25:40–29:43)**

- Hmong community's presents to Walt for helping Thao
- Sue, Thao's sister, and her mother Vu make Thao apologise to Walt
- Father Janovich's next attempt to talk to Walt

Setting 12 — **On the sidewalk (ca. 29:44–34:47)**

- Sue and boyfriend Trey harassed by group of African American teenagers
- Walt intervenes, threatening the gang with a gun, helps Sue and drives her home

Setting 13 — **In Walt's truck (ca. 34:48–36:48)**

- conversation between Sue and Walt: she tells him about the Hmong

Setting 14 — **On Walt's porch and in his house (ca. 36:49–41:57)**

- Walt's birthday: Mitch and Karen's presents are only badly veiled attempts to cart Walt off to an old people's home
- Sue invites left alone Walt to a party at their house

Setting 15 — **The Lors' house (ca. 41:58–51:41)**

- Walt introduced to guests, rituals and traditional food at party
- shaman doctor "reads" Walt quite accurately ("not at peace")
- younger people gathered in the basement of the house, Thao too shy to ask Youa out, Walt provokes him

Setting 16 | **In front of Walt's house (ca. 51:42–53:47)**

- Thao offers to work for Walt to make up for his attempt to steal Gran Torino

Setting 17 | **Inside and outside Walt's house (ca. 53:48–58:34)**

- Walt gives Thao only useless tasks
- Thao finally refurbishes houses of the neighbourhood; feels valued
- Walt coughs up blood and rudely sends Thao away

Setting 18 | **At the doctor's (ca. 58:35–59:33)**

- Walt at the doctor's

Setting 19 | **Walt's house/Mitch's house (ca. 59:34–01:01:00)**

- Walt's attempt to tell Mitch about his bad diagnosis thwarted by his son's indifference

Setting 20 | **The Lors' and Walt's houses (ca. 01:01:01–01:10:06)**

- Walt helps Thao with repair works and asks for his help in return
- closer relationship between Walt and Thao

Setting 21 | **At the barber shop (ca. 01:10:07–01:13:18)**

- Walt's attempt to "man Thao up": learning "men's talk" at Martin's barber shop

Setting 22 | **On a construction site/In a hardware store (ca. 01:13:19–01:16:46)**

- Walt helps Thao get a job on construction site and buys him equipment

Setting 23 | **In the street (ca. 01:16:47–01:19:29)**

- Spider's gang's assault on Thao

Setting 24 | **In front of the gang's house (ca. 01:19:30–01:21:23)**

- Walt beats up Smokie and tells him to leave Thao alone

Setting 25 | **Walt's garden (ca. 01:21:24–01:22:40)**

- Walt, Thao, Sue, Vu and Youa have barbecue
- Walt promises to lend Thao and Youa Gran Torino for first date

Setting 26 **The Lors' house (ca. 01:22:41–01:25:40)**

- in revenge for Walt's beating up of Smokie, gang shoots at Lors' house with semi-automatic guns, wounding Thao
- Sue returns home, badly beaten up and raped

Setting 27 **Walt's house (ca. 01:25:41–01:29:38)**

- Walt's self-blame for violence
- first open conversation between Walt and Father Janovich

Setting 28 **Walt's house (ca. 01:29:39–01:31:11)**

- Thao seeks revenge, but is sent away by Walt

Setting 29 **Walt's house, shops and church (ca. 01:31:12–01:34:37)**

- Walt gets his affairs in order: mows his lawn, has a bath, visits the barber's, buys a tailored suit, finally goes to confession (deploring his distanced relationship with his sons)

Setting 30 **Walt's house (ca. 01:34:38–01:38:39)**

- Thao locked up in the basement by Walt to prevent him from taking revenge and tarnishing his "pure" soul
- Walt brings dog Daisy to grandmother Phong

Setting 31 **In front of the gang's house (ca. 01:38:40–01:43:52)**

- Walt confronts the gang about violence against Sue and her family
- Walt's final sacrifice: provokes the gang into shooting him dead (by taking out his lighter, pretending it to be a gun) in full view of witnesses
- gang members arrested for murder of an unarmed man
- Thao and Sue watch while Walt's body is taken away

Setting 32 **In church and at a lawyer's office (ca. 01:43:53–01:46:21)**

- Walt's funeral: Thao and Sue in traditional dress; Father Janovich's personal sermon
- Walt's last will: Thao inherits Gran Torino

Setting 33 **At the shore of Lake St. Claire (ca. 01:46:22–01:47:30)**

- Thao driving the Gran Torino with Daisy sitting next to him

3 Characters

Walt Kowalski

- **nickname:** Wally (by Sue, form of endearment)
- **age:** in his 70s
- **ethnicity:** European American, descendant of Polish immigrants
- **health:** suffers from severe illness, probably lung cancer
- **job:** Korean War veteran, worked in a Ford factory
- **interests:** cars, repairing things, keeping house and garden in order, his dog Daisy, smoking, drinking
- **character traits:** self-reliant and determined, conservative and tidy-minded, grumpy, hostile and racist, conscience-stricken and lonely
- **relationship with other characters:** loving marriage with Dorothy (recently deceased), difficult relationship with his sons and their families, "manly" banter with Martin, the barber, Tim, the construction supervisor, and other drinking buddies, develops respect for Father Janovich whom he rejects and ridicules at the beginning, gradual friendship with Thao and Sue, who become like a substitute family, feels responsible for them, finally sacrifices his life for them

Thao Vang Lor

- **nickname:** Toad (by Walt, who does not make an effort to pronounce his name correctly, first an insult, then almost a form of endearment)
- **age:** about 16
- **ethnicity:** Hmong
- **job:** does not go to school, later gets a job at a construction site
- **interests:** cars, handiwork
- **character traits:** shy, self-conscious, insecure, gains self-confidence by working and through friendship with Walt
- **relationship with other characters:** lives with sister, mother, grandmother, but is not seen as "man of the house", pressured by cousin Fong to join his gang, in love with Youa, torn between two worlds of White America and traditional Hmong culture, gradually becomes friends with Walt and learns a lot from him

Sue Lor

- **age:** a little bit older than Thao
- **ethnicity:** Hmong
- **job:** goes to school/college
- **character traits:** self-confident, outspoken, intelligent, witty
- **relationship with other characters:** feels responsible for her brother, speaks up against Smokie and Spider, but gets beaten and raped by the gang, sees Walt's good heart beneath his hostile behaviour, well-adapted to American society

Father Janovich

- **age:** 27 (according to Walt)
- **ethnicity:** European American
- **job:** Catholic priest
- **interests:** his parish, philosophical questions about life and death
- **character traits:** young and inexperienced, persistent, really cares for the people in his parish
- **relationship with other characters:** was close to Dorothy Kowalski, learns a lot from Walt and gains his respect

Minor characters

- **Fong ("Spider") and Smokie:** ringleaders of violent Hmong gang, Fong is Sue and Thao's cousin
- **Mitch, Karen, Ashley and Josh Kowalski:** Walt's son and his family, difficult relationship with Walt (feel like Walt is never content with and always disappointed in them, but they are rather materialistically interested in Walt themselves)
- **Steve, wife, Daniel and David Kowalski:** Walt's other son and his family, little contact to Walt
- **Martin:** Italian-American barber, Walt's friend
- **Phong Lor:** Thao and Sue's grandmother, suspicious of American culture and rather hostile towards Walt
- **Vu Lor:** Thao and Sue's single mother, does not speak English
- **Youa:** Thao's love interest
- **Trey:** Sue's rather cowardly White boyfriend

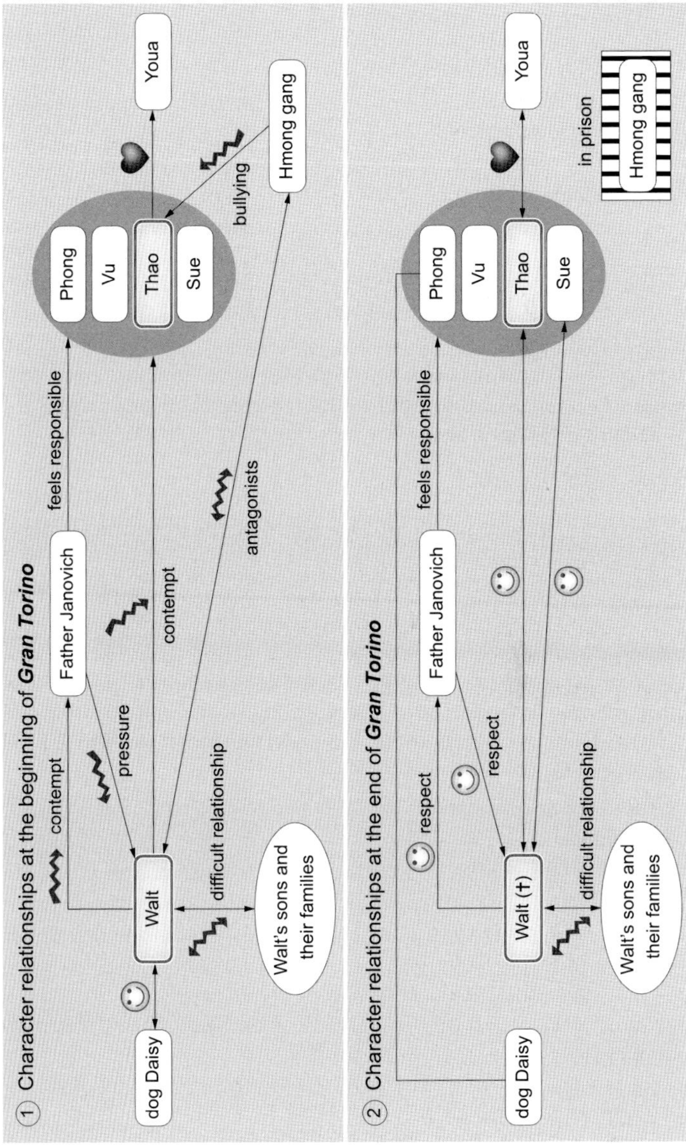
1 Character relationships at the beginning of Gran Torino
dog Daisy
Walt
Walt's sons and their families
difficult relationship
contempt
pressure
Father Janovich
feels responsible
contempt
antagonists
Phong
Vu
Thao
Sue
bullying
Hmong gang
Youa
2 Character relationships at the end of Gran Torino
dog Daisy
Walt (+)
Walt's sons and their families
difficult relationship
respect
respect
Father Janovich
feels responsible
Phong
Vu
Thao
Sue
Youa
in prison
Hmong gang

4 Themes and interpretation

The themes dealt with in *Gran Torino* relate to the topics "cultural clashes" as well as "the role of gang culture and violence".

Cultural clashes

The term "**culture**" refers to the **way of life**, especially the **values and norms** of a certain group of people. Language, religion, habits or traditions are typical cultural expressions. A **cultural clash** can arise when people with different cultural values interact. Particularly in an immigration context, but also in contexts of different age groups, genders, etc., cultural clashes can lead to a **feeling of disorientation** for the people affected.

depiction in the film

- Walt's **racism:** alienation in his neighbourhood that does not seem to exemplify his traditional values of cleanliness and order, intolerance further fed by his past as a soldier in the Korean War (had to learn to have a low opinion of Asian people in order to justify atrocities)
- role of **religion:** Father Janovich's rather shallow religiosity at the beginning in contrast to the real meaning of life and death he and Walt learn at the end (this is also assisted by Hmong shaman, who is the first to sense Walt's troubled soul)
- **generational conflict** between Walt and his sons and Walt's resulting loneliness
- Thao's **disorientation:** traditional patriarchal gender roles in Hmong culture, but difficulty for Thao to fill this role (absent father figure, no male role model to imitate until he meets Walt), harder for him to fit into American society than for Sue ("The girls go to college, the boys go to jail.")

Gang culture and violence

Disorientation often leads to young boys in particular searching for connection, belonging and a kind of substitute family in **youth gangs**. **Violence** is seen as an expression of **power** in a society where they otherwise often feel helpless and marginalised. In the USA, **gun violence** is an especially pressing problem due to the **Second Amendment** which guarantees citizens the right "to keep and bear arms". Gun ownership is often connected to "**American values**", such as independence, freedom, individualism and a kind of "frontier spirit". However, especially after mass shootings gun ownership is also discussed controversially. Witnessing or committing violence can also result in **mental health issues**, in severe cases so-called PTSD (= post-traumatic stress disorder), which manifests itself in nightmares, flashbacks and uncontrollable thoughts, but also in problems in social relationships and daily life due to emotional numbness, addiction, depressive thoughts, etc.

depiction in the film

- escalation of **violence:** insults, threats, physical violence (Smokie burning Thao with cigarette, Walt beating up Smokie, gun attack, Sue's rape, Walt provoking gang into shooting him dead)
- several gangs seem to provide **orientation** for alienated male teenagers (Hispanic, Hmong, African American); Thao's cousin tries to lure him into his gang by presenting a **wrong image of family loyalty**
- Walt probably suffering from **PTSD:** distanced relationship with other people, emotional numbness, bitterness, recurring feelings of guilt
- Walt used to solving problems through violence (war veteran and **stereotypical masculinity**), but also recognises how **violence can taint the soul**, wants Thao to stay "pure"; during his self-sacrifice, he is unarmed

Mother to Mother

1 Key facts about the novel

- **author:** Sindiwe Magona (*1943 in Gungululu, South Africa), Master's Degree in Social Work at Columbia University (USA), worked for UN Department of Public Information for about 20 years, returned to South Africa in 2003, actress, author, playwright, poet, lecturer, motivational speaker, humanitarian activist
- **year of publication:** 1998
- **adaptations:** theatre play (2009), documentary film (2020)
- **genre:** epistolary novel, fictionalised account of real-life event (murder of White American student in South African township)
- **setting:** South Africa (mainly township Guguletu near Cape Town)
- **time:** 1993 with flashbacks to the 1960s and 1970s
- **narrative perspective:** first-person narration: extended letter from Mandisa to "the girl's" mother
- **structure:** author's preface, 12 chapters: "Mandisa's lament" in chapter 1 (= letter from Mandisa, mother of "the girl's" killer, to "the girl's" mother) and interspersed throughout the novel, other chapters delineate the events leading up to and directly following the murder in non-chronological order (partly extensive flashbacks to Mandisa's youth and her early adulthood)
- **content:** Mandisa remembers the direct aftermath of "the girl's" murder and recounts her own and her son Mxolisi's life story to try and explain how he could end up killing the American student. The story is based on the case of Amy Biehl, a White American student, who spent ten months at an African university to learn about the Xhosa culture and language and helped prepare the first democratic elections in South Africa. Biehl was attacked and killed by a group of Black youths in August 1993.
- **explanation of the title:** novel is a fictional letter from the killer's to the victim's mother

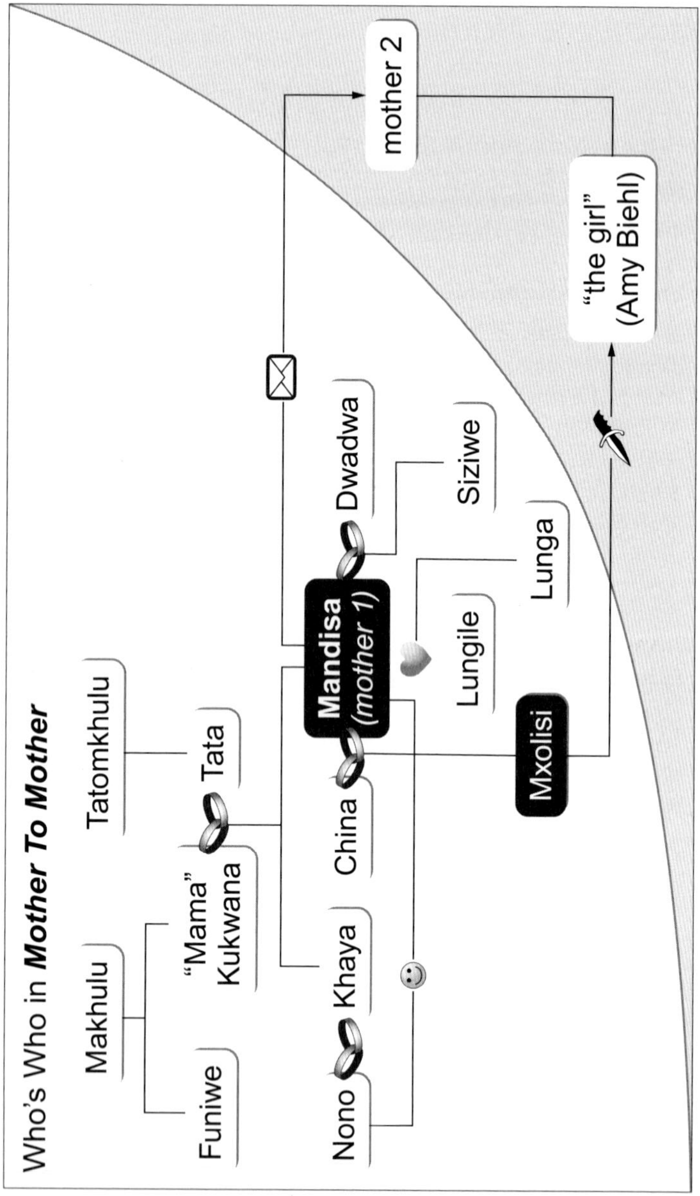
Who's Who in *Mother To Mother*
Makhulu
Tatomkhulu
Funiwe
"Mama" Kukwana
Tata
Nono
Khaya
China
Mandisa (mother 1)
Dwadwa
Siziwe
Lungile
Lunga
Mxolisi
"the girl" (Amy Biehl)
mother 2

2 Plot

Author's preface

- real-life background of the novel: Fulbright scholar Amy Biehl killed in township Guguletu in August 1993 by mob of Black youth
- novel as an attempt to gain understanding why such a cruel act could be committed and how the killers were shaped by apartheid

Chapter 1 — **Mandisa's lament**

- Mandisa's letter to "the girl's" mother: she tries to explain her son Mxolisi's murder of "the girl"
- Mandisa asks for forgiveness both for Mxolisi's deed and her own potential responsibility
- also reproaches "the girl" for visiting the Black township
- admits that she is not surprised by Mxolisi's deed and connects it to their general life circumstances
- feels like the murdered girl's mother and she herself should find common ground in their sorrow

Chapter 2 — **Mowbray – Wednesday 25 August 1993**

- juxtaposition: how Mandisa imagines "the girl's" morning on the day of her killing (her last day in South Africa) and her own morning
- Mandisa's worries about neglecting her children due to having to work and her guilty conscience for having lost control over them
- Mxolisi and his friends, who play truant as a sign of their political protest, spend their day hanging about the township, witnessing the common lootings and violence
- "the girl's" offer to drive four of her university friends home to Guguletu
- another juxtaposition of "the girl" and her friends driving into Guguletu and Mxolisi and his friends approaching her car and the commotion it causes

Chapter 3 — **5.15 p.m. – Wednesday 25 August 1993**

- Mandisa is sent home earlier than usual by her White employer, because of trouble in Guguletu

- on her way home, she experiences chaos on the bus and hears several rumours (trouble started by schoolchildren, close to Mandisa's home)
- recollection of her family being uprooted by the apartheid government and forced to move from Blouvlei to the township of Guguletu
- on returning to her house, she asks her daughter Siziwe about Mxolisi and Lunga

Chapter 4 **7.30 p.m./7.45 p.m.**

- Mandisa's reflections about her special bond with her first son Mxolisi and her bigger worries about him than her second son Lunga
- Siziwe's evasive answer as to Mxolisi's whereabouts
- next-door neighbour Skonana confirms that a White woman was stabbed by schoolchildren close to their homes, which will lead to big trouble with the police

Chapter 5 **[–]/10.05 p.m.**

- Mandisa recalls happy memories of her family's home in Blouvlei, from where they were forced to move to Guguletu when Mandisa was nine years old
- talk of relocation starts as a rumour, but becomes reality by plane dropping off flyers
- despite all protests and appeals to parliament, Mandisa's family and neighbours are driven out by the army and police vehicles while bulldozers destroy their tin shacks
- back in 1993, Mandisa is really anxious about the situation in Guguletu as Mxolisi has not returned home
- Dwadwa comes home and expresses his view that Mxolisi will give them trouble, Mandisa feels like her husband blames her for not being able to control her son
- Mandisa recollects incidents similar to "the girl's" fatal encounter: Belgian nurses, protesting against apartheid, beaten up by African men, nun who was also trying to help killed as well
- Mandisa attributes these incidents to a lack of education as well as a general desensitisation to and even glorification of violence towards White people in the townships
- addressing "the girl's" mother directly, Mandisa once again wonders why the latter's daughter has not kept away from Guguletu

Chapter 6 **4 a.m. – Thursday 26 August 1993**

- violent police raid at Mandisa's home: police are looking for Mxolisi
- as they do not know his whereabouts, the police beat Mandisa, Lunga and Dwadwa and tear up their home

Chapter 7 **[–]/Gungululu September 1972**

- flashback to 1972: Mandisa's mother worries about unwanted pregnancy and regularly checks whether her daughter still is a virgin
- Mandisa and her boyfriend China do not have penetrative sex
- when Mandisa's friend Nono gets pregnant from Mandisa's brother Khaya and Mandisa refuses to have monthly virginity checks, she is forced to live with her grandmother Makhulu in Gungululu, a remote village in the Transkei
- her grandmother is kind to her, but Mandisa misses China and looks forward to a visit from her aunt Funiwe, who she believes might take her to East London (South Africa)
- Funiwe discovers that Mandisa is pregnant, which comes as a shock to both Mandisa and her mother

Chapter 8

- Mandisa is brought back to Cape Town, kept prisoner in her own house, ignored by her father and forbidden any contact with China
- eventually, China visits her, but is terrified on discovering that she is expecting a baby (his future plans are destroyed by the pregnancy and he does not want to believe he is the father)
- after dire negotiations, China's family agrees that the teenagers should get married
- Mxolisi (original name: "Hlumelo") born in January 1973
- Mandisa first hates him for disrupting her life, but also feels overwhelming love for her baby
- Mandisa does not want to marry China any longer, but has to bow to the families' wishes: she and Mxolisi are renamed, she has to work in the household of China's family and is denied further education
- when China disappears for good one day, she works as a domestic help and raises Mxolisi as a single mother

- at the age of four, Mxolisi betrays two older boys (Zazi and Mzamo) by telling the police about their hiding place; when his two friends are shot dead, Mxolisi refuses to talk for two years
- Mandisa meets Lungile, who gets on well with Mxolisi
- when her second son Lunga is born, Mxolisi starts wetting the bed and wants to know where his own father is
- Lungile crosses the border to train as a freedom fighter and the family has great difficulties trying to make ends meet: Mxolisi offers to leave school and start working but is persuaded to stay in high school, where he gets involved in politics
- Mandisa marries Dwadwa and her daughter Siziwe is born
- Mxolisi becomes a hero in the neighbourhood and is praised for his decency (e. g. saving a girl from being raped)

Chapter 9 **6 a.m. – Thursday 26 August**

- after the police raid: Mandisa suspects more and more that Mxolisi might be involved in the White girl's murder, Lunga's cuts and bruises are only superficial, but Siziwe seems to be badly hurt in a psychological way
- she tells her mother that Mxolisi came home shortly before the police raid and might have hidden something in the boys' hut
- Mandisa stays home from work in case Mxolisi returns

Chapter 10 **[–]/1 p.m. – Thursday 26 August**

- Mandisa remembers her grandfather telling her how White colonialism negatively impacted the Xhosa people (e. g. cattle killing as an attempt to get rid of the foreign settlers) and how a hatred of White people was ingrained in her from early on
- Mandisa begins her search of Mxolisi, following a hint by the same Anglican priest who has refused Mxolisi and his friends the use of his church for a political gathering earlier
- Mandisa eventually finds her son in a hiding place
- she does not get a conclusive answer whether he killed "the girl" or not (he stresses that there were several killers involved)
- although Mxolisi repeatedly tells his mother that he did not kill "the girl", she does not believe him and knows that he will be arrested; she still consoles him

Chapter 11 **[–]/Guguletu, much later**

- Mandisa directly addresses "the girl's" mother as her "Sister-Mother", wonders what to do about Mxolisi now and tries to explain the political background behind "the girl's" death
- she feels sorrow for the victim's mother but also pities herself and her family, as she feels like an outcast in her community
- she cannot understand why her son was singled out from the crowd as the murderer of the White student and sees political leaders as the real culprits
- later on, her neighbours grieve with her and she finds hope in this act of solidarity
- resuming the conversation with "the girl's" mother, she claims that she feels close to her in sorrow, but at least the other mother does not need to feel ashamed

Chapter 12 **[–]/Guguletu, late afternoon Wednesday 25 August**

- Mandisa deplores the hopelessness in Mxolisi's young life and his "lost generation"
- in the format of an eye-witness report, Mandisa finally gives an account of what happened on Wednesday, 25 August 1993
- beginning where she left off in chapter two, with "the girl's" yellow Mazda entering Guguletu, Mxolisi and his gang are reported walking the streets after being refused the use of the Anglican church hall for their gathering
- as soon as the mob recognises a White person behind the Mazda's steering wheel, the car is rocked and the slogan "one settler, one bullet" shows that "the girl" is singled out because she is White
- the situation gets out of control, stones are thrown and people get more and more violent
- Mandisa blames herself and her community for what happened: she claims that their children have been encouraged to seek revenge for the atrocities caused by apartheid and that her own son is "only an agent executing the long-simmering dark desires of his race"

Chronology of Events in ***Mother to Mother***		
1968	**1972**	**1973**
forced removal of Mandisa's family from Blouvlei to Guguletu	Mandisa has to live with her grandmother in Gugululu	Mxolisi's birth and Mandisa's marriage to China

1977		**1993**
police shooting of Zazi and Mzamo	Mxolisi's political radicalisation	killing of "the girl" in Guguletu

3 Characters

Mandisa

- other name: Nohehake (renamed by first husband China's family)
- **in her 30s** at the time of "the girl's" murder
- **mother of three** and **very hard worker**
- as a girl, **obedient**, **respectful**, **hardworking**, **promising student**
- has had to face several hardships in her life: **dislocation** at 9, **unwanted pregnancy** at 15, **loveless marriage**, **single motherhood**, **poverty and discrimination**
- **values education** (especially because her own was cut short by her unexpected pregnancy)
- seems to care a great deal about **her children** and feels responsible for their deeds
- **complicated relationship to Mxolisi:** resents him for "taking away her virginity" and destroying her educational prospects, also loves him deeply and feels connected to him because they spent so much time alone together
- **feels helpless** and overwhelmed by Mxolisi's uncontrollability **and** generally **guilty** for not being a good enough mother

Mxolisi

- other names: Hlumelo, Michael
- **20** at the time of "the girl's" murder, recently circumcised (symbol of being a man)
- **special relationship to his mother:** early "rejection", but now particularly close
- in his young life experienced **many losses:** both his father and his mother's boyfriend Lungile left the family, he lost two friends when he gave away their hiding place during a police raid and refused to speak for a while (**childhood trauma/guilt**)
- at age 20, at educational level of a young teenager although he is **very intelligent** (top student as long as he goes to school)
- however, **stubborn and headstrong** and described as rather lazy by his stepfather Dwadwa

- **disoriented**, no future prospects
- **political activism** and deep-seated resentments against White people
- **multi-faceted** character: **righteous anger**, callous and **desensitised to violence**, murders an innocent student and denies responsibility for his deed, but also **sensitive and helpful person**, saved a young girl from being raped and was willing to leave school to contribute to the family income

Siziwe

- Mandisa's **third child and only girl**, only biological child of Dwadwa
- badly affected by police raid
- sometimes **jealous** of Mxolisi's special treatment, but also **loyal** towards him

Lunga

- **14** at the time of "the girl's" murder
- Mandisa's **second son** from a short relationship with the later freedom fighter Lungile
- the "**reader**" **of the family**, Mandisa sees him as rather soft, not as politically active as his brother

Dwadwa

- Siziwe's biological father and Mandisa's current partner
- seems to be a **good provider for his family**, cares for all three children, but does not seem to feel responsible for Mxolisi
- **steadfast**, rather simple-minded, in comparison to Mandisa's constant worries, **rather carefree**

"the girl" (Amy Biehl)

- never explicitly called Amy Biehl, but **based on the White Fulbright student**, who came from New York to Cape Town to study Xhosa culture and language and help people prepare for the first free elections in post-apartheid South Africa
- happy, optimistic, **carefree**, **idealistic**, altruistic, innocent, **naive**

China

- **Mandisa's first boyfriend** and **Mxolisi's father**
- **excellent student**
- as Mandisa's boyfriend, **considerate and affectionate**, does not pressure her to have sex with him
- turns out to be a big disappointment because he is **not willing to accept his role as a father**, denies any responsibility for his child
- eventually agrees to go through with the marriage, but takes out his **frustration** (of not being able to pursue his education and being forced to work instead) on Mandisa
- **self-centred** (even indicates that he would have preferred an abortion, revealing how little he cares about either Mandisa or Mxolisi)
- finally **disappears**, leaving his young wife and child

Kukwana "Mama"

- Mandisa and her brother Khaya's mother
- **firm and strict**, but also **loving**
- active in the local church, obsessed with Mandisa's virginity (but mainly because she wants her daughter to have chances, she **values education highly**)
- **traditional view** of the girl being the responsible party in case of an unwanted pregnancy
- very disappointed in Mandisa after she finds out about her pregnancy, but learns to love Mxolisi deeply and to forgive Mandisa

4 Themes and interpretation

The themes dealt with in *Mother to Mother* relate to the major topics "ethnic and cultural diversity", "apartheid in South Africa" and "accountability and justice".

Ethnic and cultural diversity

South Africa is known for its **ethnic and cultural diversity**, which is also reflected in its nickname, "The Rainbow Nation", and its motto, translated to "Unity in Diversity". For many years, however, life in South Africa was characterised by the **domination of a White minority over the Black majority**, with a strict separation of different ethnic groups and exploitation of the Indigenous population. The **legacy of the apartheid regime** (cf. "Apartheid in South Africa") is still evident in **large disparities** between Black and White people's standards of living as well as a **deep-rooted mistrust** of one another, which is one of the main topics of Magona's novel. As Mandisa, the narrator and protagonist of *Mother to Mother*, belongs to the **Xhosa people**, the novel allows the reader an insight into this culture.

Background information

17th to 19th century	– **1652:** trading post by **Dutch East India Company** established in Cape Town – **1795/1806: British** seize the **Cape Colony** from the Dutch – both Dutch and British settlers **displace and suppress the Indigenous population** – **1856/1857: Xhosa cattle killing**
19th and early 20th century	– **end of 19th century: diamond and gold discoveries**, which attracted **more settlers** and pushed the **Indigenous peoples** further back; many of them became **dependent on the "European" economy** and had to work in low-paid jobs in mines etc. – **Anglo-Boer Wars** (1880–1902) resulted in **British sovereignty** – **1910: Union of South Africa** founded as an **independent** state – **segregation and discrimination against Black majority** codified by several acts (Black people excluded from skilled jobs, prevented from owning land, restricted in their movement through pass laws, etc.) – **1948:** official beginning of **apartheid** era

depiction in the novel

- **different versions of history:** cattle killings as act of stupidity ("White master narrative") vs. act of desperation (Tatomkhulu)
- Mandisa's family **between traditional Xhosa culture** (role of the family, marriage rites, etc.) **and** (**negative**) **colonial influence** (dependence on money, hard work in low-paid jobs, neglecting parents' responsibilities)
- Mandisa's mother: very strict and traditional in her attitude to sexuality, but also influenced by her desire to make a better life / education possible for Mandisa
- **role of women:** blamed for pregnancies, slave-like working for in-laws
- **cohesion and solidarity** threatened by relocations, but still important for Mandisa's family (e. g. grieving together with neighbours)

Apartheid in South Africa

Officially introduced in **1948**, the policy of apartheid was valid in South Africa until the **first free elections in 1994** with Nelson Mandela becoming the first democratic president of the country. Apartheid is characterised by the official **legislation of discriminatory and segregationist practices**. Black and other non-White people were not allowed to vote and subject to various forms of discrimination, such as the prohibition of "mixed marriages", the segregation of public facilities, a severely limited education, restrictions on the type of jobs they were allowed to work in and strict housing and settlement laws. Apartheid finally ended due to a combination of **inner resistance**, armed struggle and underground activity as well as **international opposition** and sanctions against South Africa. However, the aftermath of decades of oppression and disadvantages can still be felt. A tense, often violent relationship between non-White and White South Africans is one result.

Background information

1948	(Afrikaner) **National Party** wins elections: **apartheid** is officially introduced
1960	**ANC** (African National Congress) and **ANCYL** (African National Congress Youth League = "Young Lions") **banned**

1961	South Africa becomes a **republic** and is more or less **forced to leave the Commonwealth** (resistance to apartheid system by other member states)
1976	**Soweto uprising:** demonstrations and protests by Black schoolchildren against Afrikaans as language of instruction; crushed with violence, many casualties
1977	"Black Consciousness" leader **Steve Biko** dies in police custody: new waves of protest, world's attention focused on South African state
1986	**worldwide sanctions** put into effect against South Africa
1990	**Nelson Mandela's release** after 27 years in prison; State President F.W. de Klerk **set to dismantle apartheid**
1990–1994	South African government and ANC negotiate **ending minority rule**
1994	**first free and democratic elections:** Mandela becomes president and de Klerk his deputy president
1996	first hearings of Truth and Reconciliation Commission (**TRC**)

depiction in the novel

- novel shows political situation and social conditions both in apartheid (flashbacks) and post-apartheid South Africa
- the **forced removal** of Mandisa's whole community from Blouvlei to Guguletu in the 1960s, the fact that there are not enough housing and schooling facilities for the people in the new township and the loss of the family's source of income show the **negative economic and social impact** of the relocations ("The afterbirths of our children are deep in this ground. So are […] the bleached bones of our long dead.", Chapter 5)
- Guguletu = "Our Pride" renamed Gugulabo = "Their Pride" by the inhabitants (**pretence vs. reality**)
- common **violence** (e. g. "necklacing") and deep-seated **hatred** as answers to **powerlessness**, **frustration** and **lawlessness** in townships
- **Operation Barcelona** (organised by COSAS/Congress of South African Students) as an example of youth protest against inadequate education, but also compounds the problem
- increasing frustration, especially felt by the younger generation, leads to **political radicalisation**, as shown in the slogans "one settler, one bullet", "Power! It is ours!", "Boers, they are dogs!"
- hopelessness, discrimination and ingrained hatred as real reasons for "the girl's" murder

Accountability and justice

Undoubtedly, *Mother to Mother* deals with a hideous crime, the murder of an innocent young student. However, the **murderer** Mxolisi could also be seen as a **victim**. According to his mother, he belongs to a **lost generation**. In Mandisa's opinion, his deed must be seen in a wider context of guilt and responsibility. Sindiwe Magona portrays how closely **apartheid and violence** are connected in South Africa's history and how difficult it is to find **reconciliation** between White and non-White South Africans.

Background information

The Truth and Reconciliation Commission (TRC)	– goal/aim: **national reconciliation** – **platform for both victims and perpetrators** to speak about the crimes they suffered from or committed – possibility to gain **amnesty** for perpetrating crimes (real-life murderers of Amy Biehl were granted amnesty) – hope for a fuller understanding of the past and a new, more peaceful beginning – generally seen as a **success**

depiction in the novel

- individual guilt explained in terms of **collective retaliation and deferred responsibilities**
- in her conversation with "the girl's" mother, Mandisa claims that her son fell victim to the political climate he was born into
- Mxolisi grew up in a society that hated "the Whites" in general and even applauded first spurts of violence by young people
- Mandisa also struggles with her own responsibility: she feels blamed for Mxolisi's deed and acknowledges that she *is* responsible; yet, her lack of time for her children and her inability to control them is also attributed to larger societal roots
- Mandisa's ray of hope: her neighbours come to her house to grieve with her, she does not feel like an outsider anymore; **communication** is key for her → that is why she writes to "the girl's" mother and gives testimony to the whole prehistory of the murder (wants to create a connection/common ground/share their sorrows)

Frankenstein

1 Key facts about the novel

- **author:** Mary Wollstonecraft Shelley (1797–1851), daughter of political writer William Godwin and feminist writer/activist Mary Wollstonecraft, married Romantic poet Percy Bysshe Shelley in 1816, husband drowned in 1822
- **year of publication:** 1818 (first edition), 1831 (revised edition)
- **adaptations:** numerous literary, film and musical adaptations, also computer games, comics, toys, Halloween costumes, etc. (one of the most popular film versions is the 1931 film with Boris Karloff as the Monster)
- **genre:** gothic novel, romantic novel, science-fiction novel
- **setting:** Switzerland, France, Italy, Germany, England, Scotland, Ireland, Russia, North Pole
- **time:** 18th century
- **narrative perspective:** epistolary novel; three first-person narrators: explorer Robert Walton, Victor Frankenstein, the Monster
- **structure:** Introduction (1831), Preface (1818), 4 letters, 24 chapters, 5 final letters
- **content:** Victor Frankenstein constructs the semblance of a human being from stolen body parts; physically ugly but good-natured, the Monster turns evil because people and Frankenstein reject him. After the Monster kills Frankenstein's brother, friend and wife, the scientist pursues him to the North Pole, where they both perish.
- **explanation of title:** *Frankenstein:* name of the scientist; complete title: *Frankenstein; or, the Modern Prometheus*; *Prometheus:* a Titan in Greek mythology, who created human beings from clay, stole fire and gave it to humanity, represents quest for knowledge and defiance of the gods

Background information

gothic novel	– subcategory of **romanticism** – (supernatural) elements of **horror and death** – "the **sublime**": extraordinary experiences and **emotions**, **nature** in its grandeur and terror
romantic novel	– protagonists with **strong individual emotions** – glorious **nature**
science-fiction novel	– deals with an **imagined** (so far) unrealistic **future** – based on **scientific or technological innovations**

Narrators in ***Frankenstein***

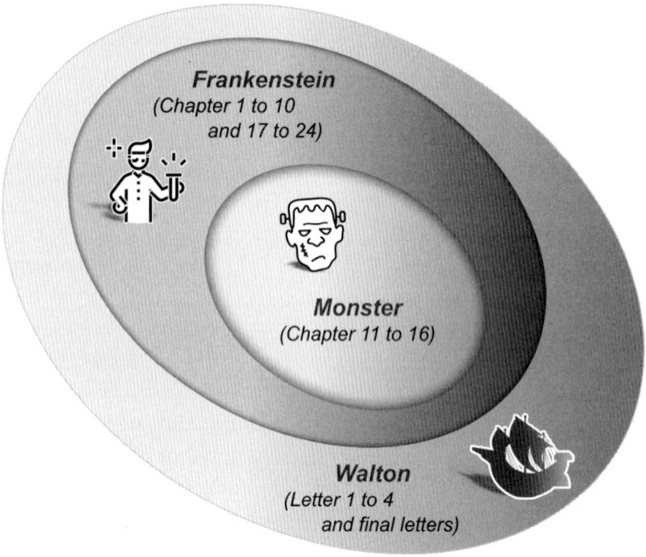

2 Plot

Introduction (1831) and Preface (1818)

- Mary Shelley explains the origin of her novel
- contest between her, her husband and Byron to write a ghost story during a wet summer in Switzerland
- scientific considerations ("galvanism") and misuse of knowledge at the basis of her story

Letters 1 to 4

narrator: Robert Walton who writes to his sister Margaret Saville in England

Letter 1 | **St. Petersburgh, Dec. 11, 17xx**

- explorer Walton informs his sister about his plan for a voyage to the North Pole

Letter 2 | **Archangel, March 28, 17xx**

- Walton feels lonely but is still set on finding a ship and gathering men for his expedition

Letter 3 | **July 7, 17xx**

- Walton starts on his journey, full of optimism and confidence

Letter 4 | **August 5, 17xx; August 13, 17xx; August 19, 17xx**

- crew members observe huge savage figure (the Monster)
- Victor Frankenstein's rescue from drowning in icy waters
- Frankenstein's promise to tell his story

Chapters 1 to 10

narrator: Victor Frankenstein

Chapter 1

- Victor's happy childhood in Italy and Geneva (Switzerland) with loving parents Alphonse and Caroline Frankenstein
- the family adopt a beautiful orphan girl, Elizabeth Lavenza

Chapter 2

- happy childhood with Elizabeth and his schoolmate Henry Clerval
- intent on explaining the secrets of nature, he studies "natural philosophy"
- focuses on ancient occult scientists (Cornelius Agrippa, Albertus Magnus, Paracelsus)
- their imperfection and outdatedness and the realisation that knowledge in the natural sciences will always remain incomplete makes Victor turn to mathematics instead

Chapter 3

- at age 17, Victor loses his mother, who dies of scarlet fever
- leaves Geneva to study at Ingolstadt university
- meets M. Krempe, professor of natural philosophy, and M. Waldman, professor of chemistry
- Waldman ignites Victor's ambition to "unfold to the world the deepest mysteries of creation"

Chapter 4

- Victor as an ardent and very successful student
- full concentration on "bestowing animation on lifeless matter" (Victor collects material in mortuaries, dissecting rooms and slaughterhouses)
- enthusiasm turns to obsession, unhealthy ignorance of life and social contacts as well as anxiety and nervousness

Chapter 5

- Frankenstein brings the Monster to life
- horrified by his creation's ugliness, he flees from his laboratory and later his bedchamber where the Monster has followed him
- runs into Henry Clerval
- afraid of returning to his apartment and of Clerval finding the Monster, Victor is relieved to find his creation gone
- Victor falls ill with a nervous fever for several months
- Henry nurses him back to health; Victor refuses to tell him the truth

Chapter 6

- letter from Elizabeth: Justine Moritz, a former servant of the family, has returned to the household
- Victor introduces Henry to his professors, but suffers from being reminded of natural sciences
- Victor and Henry out on a tour around Ingolstadt

Chapter 7

- Victor's younger brother William has been killed
- on inspecting the spot of the murder, Victor sees the Monster and believes him responsible for the killing
- Justine, the housemaid, is accused of the young boy's murder because his locket is found on her

Chapter 8

- at the trial Victor cannot help Justine, because he thinks nobody would believe his story anyway
- Justine is sentenced to death and executed
- Victor's despair and remorse

Chapter 9

- Victor is distraught and thinks of taking his life
- feels responsibility for William's and Justine's deaths, but also hatred towards the Monster
- on a journey to the valley of Chamounix, he experiences short moments of relief

Chapter 10

- Victor climbs a mountain and suddenly sees the Monster advancing on him
- the Monster explains he turned from benevolence to wickedness because Victor and his fellow creatures despised and rejected him
- he demands that Victor listen to his story

Chapters 11 to 16

narrator: the Monster

Chapter 11

- gradual development of his senses after waking up and finding himself abandoned
- first contact with other human beings: frightened reactions, Monster is chased from a village
- hiding in a shed behind a cottage from where he watches a family and their daily routine (De Lacey family: blind father, son Felix, daughter Agatha)

Chapter 12

- Monster admires the family's kindness and wants to get in contact with them
- he notices the De Laceys' unhappiness and poverty and secretly helps them by no longer stealing their food and providing them with wood
- seeing his own reflection in a pool, the Monster is shocked by his ugly appearance
- wants to master language in order not to scare the De Laceys away
- calls them his "protectors" (naive hope for their affection)

Chapter 13

- Safie, an "Arabian" woman and Felix's lover, arrives
- as she cannot speak French, Felix teaches her; the Monster profits from these lessons as well, learns the language and acquires knowledge of history and society

- with his increasing knowledge, the Monster also becomes more and more desperate because of his isolation and singularity

Chapter 14

- eventful history of the De Lacey family revealed: exiled from higher society and thrown into poverty because of their attempt to support Safie's father, who later deceived them
- instead of marrying Safie to Felix, her father intended to escape with her to Constantinople; Safie manages to come to the De Laceys' place of exile in Germany instead

Chapter 15

- in the neighbouring wood the Monster finds three books, *Paradise Lost*, *Plutarch's Lives* and *The Sorrows of Werther*
- learns new values about virtues and vices, identifies with the unrequited love of Goethe's *Werther* and sees parallels as well as differences between himself and Adam as well as Satan in *Paradise Lost*
- learns from Victor's notes about his coming into being and curses both his creation and his creator
- reveals himself to blind father when the rest of the family is out
- has a conversation with the blind man and even arouses his sympathy until the others return
- attacked by Felix, he manages to escape to his hovel

Chapter 16

- the shocked family leaves the cottage and the Monster burns it down
- enraged he makes his way to Geneva to take revenge on Frankenstein
- on the way, he saves a little girl from drowning, but her horrified father shoots at him in return
- wants to kidnap Victor's little brother William to alleviate his loneliness, but ends up killing him when he reveals his relationship to Frankenstein
- removes locket from the dead body and puts it into the dress of Justine, who is sleeping nearby

- the Monster demands Frankenstein create a female companion "of the same species" for him

Chapters 17 to 24

narrator: Victor Frankenstein

Chapter 17

- although Victor is somehow moved by the Monster's story, he does not want to become guilty again in creating another monster
- as the Monster promises to leave human beings forever as soon as he has a companion, Victor eventually agrees

Chapter 18

- Victor has second thoughts about fulfilling the Monster's wish and is at the same time afraid of his revenge
- unable to overcome his moral scruples, he hesitates and is torn between deep depression and moments of hope
- his father suggests that Victor and Elizabeth should get married
- Victor asks to postpone the celebration until he has completed further studies in England
- accompanied by his friend Henry Clerval, he travels along the Rhine

Chapter 19

- in London, Victor is still deeply in doubt about the project but tries to obtain more information for the completion of his promise
- feels a stark contrast between his own gloom and Henry's optimism
- on invitation Victor and Henry travel to Scotland but eventually separate
- Victor wants to be alone to set up a laboratory on the Orkneys and start work on a new creature

Chapter 20

- while Victor is still deliberating whether to proceed with his labour, he sees the Monster looking in through the window of his lab
- horrified by his sight, he destroys his work

- the Monster returns vowing revenge ("I shall be with you on your wedding-night")
- before resuming his travels with Clerval, Victor wants to remove the traces of his work and dumps the body parts in the sea
- his boat is washed ashore in Ireland where he is accused of having committed a murder

Chapter 21

- the murdered man turns out to be Victor's friend Henry
- Victor is sure that the Monster was the killer and sinks into a fever again
- he convinces the magistrate of his innocence, is acquitted and decides to return to Geneva with his father, who has come to Ireland
- often thinks about killing himself, but feels duty-bound to look after his family

Chapter 22

- Victor and his father interrupt their voyage in Paris for Victor to recover and regain strength, but he shuns society because he feels he deserves no part in it
- Victor accuses himself of being the murderer of William, Justine and Henry, but does not disclose the Monster's existence in front of his father
- he and Elizabeth exchange letters and set the wedding date
- back home in Switzerland, the ceremony is performed, and the couple go on honeymoon to Lake Como
- Victor is heavily armed (pistols and dagger) to defend himself because he suspects the Monster will attack him in his wedding night

Chapter 23

- instead, Elizabeth is murdered in their room
- Victor sees the Monster, fires his pistol at him but misses
- he rushes back to Geneva, where his father dies on hearing the news of Elizabeth's death
- as he does not receive any help from the magistrate for hunting down the Monster, Victor vows to spend his life chasing and destroying his enemy

Chapter 24

- Victor is miserable and completely obsessed with his mission for revenge
- on his pursuit of the Monster towards the North Pole, Victor is rescued from a piece of ice by Captain Walton
- he implores Walton to seek the Monster and take revenge should he, Victor, die

Walton's final letters

narrator: Robert Walton

August 26th, September 2d, 5th, 7th, 12th

- enclosed by ice, Walton's men implore him to return to England as soon as possible
- Frankenstein appeals to their ambition
- however, Frankenstein is weak and desperate and finally dies (sad for Walton who regards him as a friend and noble man)
- the Monster reappears grieving over Victor's coffin
- he laments his loneliness and describes himself as a "fallen angel" who became "a malignant devil" because nobody loved and accepted him
- he jumps on his ice-raft, intent on taking his life by burning himself
- Walton eventually abandons his quest for the North Pole

3 Characters

Victor Frankenstein

- oldest son of the Frankenstein family, **happy childhood** in a wealthy family
- **sensitive**, **intelligent**, **passionate** and **ambitious** scientist, smitten with the **thirst for knowledge**
- disgusted by his own creation; in deep **remorse** of his achievement and guilt for the deaths of loved ones
- **isolation** and **secrecy** as results
- **depression** and **melancholy** turn to **obsession with revenge**
- **ambivalent** whether he is a **positive or negative character:** strong feelings and morals, pays a high price for his thirst for knowledge and ambition, but ultimately responsible for Monster's depravity

The Monster

- **superhuman** size, strength and speed
- **hideous outer appearance** (composed of dead body parts), but originally **kind** and **sensitive**
- **embittered** by people's rejection, he turns into a **merciless killer**
- **blames his creator** Victor for his utter loneliness and seeks **revenge**
- ultimately feels **remorse** and mourns Victor's death
- decides to take his own life to end the disastrous development
- another **ambivalent** character: **noble impulses** (saving girl from drowning, helping the De Laceys), turns to **evil murderer**, but only because of **desperation**, **rejection** and **loneliness**, could be seen as tragic victim or cruel villain

Robert Walton

- **ambitious explorer**, caring brother, affectionate and interested listener
- knows **loneliness** and is **in search of a friend**
- similar to Victor: on **quest for new horizons** (Arctic passage)
- similarly determined to achieve his aim against resistance, but eventually **admits his failure and abandons his plan**

Elizabeth Lavenza

- **orphan** adopted by Frankenstein family, later **Victor's wife**
- **pretty**, **pleasant**, loved by everyone
- **caring**, **compassionate**, **sensitive lover of nature**
- from feminist perspective criticised as a **rather passive character**

Henry Clerval

- **Victor's life-long friend** and favourite companion
- **sensitive lover of nature** and **enthusiastic university student** (at first obliged to assist his father, a merchant, later allowed to study)
- **loyal and caring** (travel companion, nurses Victor during illness)
- his **optimism** and **sense of adventure** in stark contrast to Victor's bouts of brooding depression

Alphonse Frankenstein

- **devoted husband** of orphaned Caroline Beaufort (who later dies of scarlet fever)
- **caring and loving father** of three sons (William, Ernest, Victor)
- wealthy, honoured and respected public officer; later travels with his young family
- not particularly interested in sciences
- concerned about Victor's health
- dies of grief on hearing of Elizabeth's murder

William Frankenstein

- **Victor's youngest brother**, dearly loved by his family
- innocent **first victim of the Monster**

Justine Moritz

- well-liked **servant** in Frankenstein household
- **dutiful and caring**
- **wrongfully accused** as William's killer
- at first desperate, but dies peacefully because of her **certainty of being innocent**

De Lacey family

- blind father, son Felix and daughter Agatha, later Felix's "Arabian" lover Safie
- undeservedly **poor**, but **honest and kind** people
- however, **prejudiced** against the Monster's ugly appearance

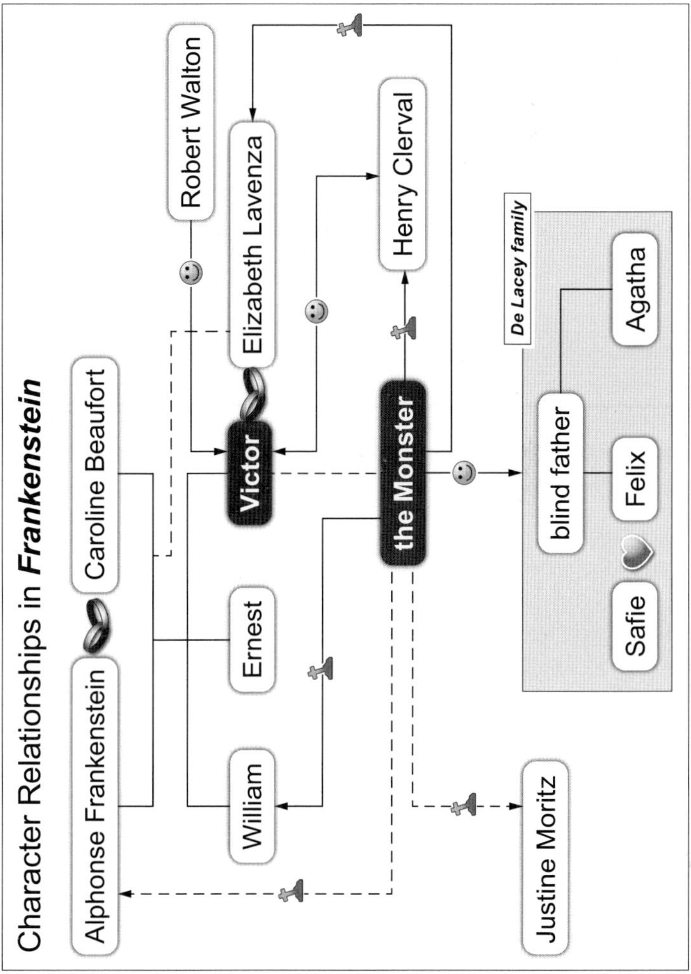

4 Themes and interpretation

Background information	
Paradise Lost **(1667)**	**author:** John Milton (1608–1674) **form:** epic poem in 12 books **theme:** the rebellion of Satan and his followers against God, the rebellion of Adam and Eve against divine law in the Garden of Eden **connection with novel *Frankenstein:*** Frankenstein as ambitious as Satan, Monster identifies both with Adam (suffering from loneliness) and Satan ("the fallen angel")
Plutarch's Lives **(ca. 100)**	**author:** Plutarch (ca. 45–125) **form:** 48 biographies of famous men **theme:** Greek and Roman men's lives juxtaposed to reveal their virtues and vices **connection with novel *Frankenstein:*** the Monster's source to learn about good and bad
Sorrows of Werther **(1774)**	**author:** Johann Wolfgang Goethe (1749–1832) **form:** epistolary novel **theme:** young Werther falls in love with engaged Charlotte and commits suicide out of despair **connection with novel *Frankenstein:*** Monster learns about deep emotions from the novel, can identify with Werther's experience of unrequited love and also plans to commit suicide at the end

Ethics of science

Mary Shelley's *Frankenstein* is regarded as one of the forerunners of what became known as "**dystopian science fiction**" – a view of a potentially intimidating future development. In her story she explores the **limits of science and technology** and illustrates how scientists can go wrong and too far. Today these ethical issues are more relevant than ever. In connection with advanced methods of genetic engineering, in particular, there have been controversial discussions as to whether everything that is possible should also be allowed or whether there might be **unintended and uncontrollable detrimental repercussions** of all the scientific and/or technological potential being unleashed.

depiction in the novel

- the erroneous concept of unrestricted freedom of science:
  - as a student Victor follows Professor Waldman's misguided conviction that there is **no limit to scientific research** and science will almost always turn out for the best: "The labours of men of genius, however erroneously directed, scarcely ever fail in ultimately turning to the solid advantage of mankind." (Chapter 3)
  - after his first successful experiments, Victor feels satisfaction and expects gratitude and ultimately a way to conquer death (**God complex**) ("A new species would bless me as its creator and source […]. No father could claim the gratitude of his child so completely as I should deserve theirs. […] I might in process of time […] renew life where death had apparently devoted the body to corruption.", Chapter 4)
  - Victor's work is seen as "**playing God**" and his **secrecy** throughout the process shows that he ultimately knows that what he does is wrong
- the repercussions of unrestricted science:
  - the Monster is more or less **uncontrollable** because he is stronger than human beings
  - Victor is **responsible for the misery of his creature**, whom he abandons, and the **deaths of innocent people**
  - he has also **destroyed his own life:** "Cursed (although I curse myself) be the hands that formed you! You have made me wretched beyond expression." (Chapter 10)
  - he admits he was **blind to the consequences** of his actions: "my eyes were shut to the horror of my proceedings." (Chapter 19)
- the responsibility of scientists:
  - Victor **shunning the responsibility** for his creature
  - Victor does **not divulge his knowledge** towards Walton because he knows of its catastrophic results and wants to **prevent him from repeating his mistakes**
  - he destroys his second project (companion for the Monster) for fears of his creation completely **spiralling out of control**
  - the explorer Robert Walton represents the **responsible scientist** who gives up his quest to save the lives of his men

Role of nature

Mary Shelley and her husband Percy lived and wrote during the literary age termed Romanticism (ca. 1770–1848). The **Romantic Movement** was a strong reaction to the **Age of Reason** (Enlightenment) of the 18th century which focused on **rationality and thought**. Romantic artists were driven by **imagination**, **emotion**, **passion** and the **love of nature**. Lord Byron, a close friend of the Shelleys, wrote "I love not Man the less, but Nature more", and the American poet Henry David Thoreau stated, "In the wilderness is the salvation of the world".

depiction in the novel

- nature is the greatest mysterious force in the universe:
  - many scenes take place in settings where the **grandeur of nature** makes people feel awestruck (Alps, Orkney Islands, North Pole)
  - Victor aims at **discovering the secrets of nature**, but his **arrogant ambition** has dangerous and unforeseen consequences
  - nature is perfect, whereas people are faulty
- the beauty of nature elates and provides **consolation**, eases pain
  - following unpleasant or disturbing experiences Victor finds relief in nature
  - even the Monster feels consoled by springtime

Questions of (human) identity

In the depiction of its two main characters, Victor Frankenstein and his Monster, the novel *Frankenstein* seems to question common definitions of humanity. What makes us human and are we allowed to **deny humanity** to creatures just because they are **different**? Is it not rather a sign of real monstrosity or villainy to deprive other beings of the **basic needs of community, recognition and affection**?

depiction in the novel

- theme of **loneliness:** Victor turns from happy member of society to obsessed scientist and finally to gloomy and disturbed outsider, Walton is lonely and wants to find a friend, the Monster's chief emotion is one of rejection and loneliness

- role of **family:** the Monster listens to De Lacey family and searches for his own connections, he wants a female companion to ease his solitude, his revenge consists in making Frankenstein as lonely as he is (stripping away all his family ties)
- the **pain of not being accepted:** the Monster's whole history is one of trying to belong to society and being shunned and rejected for his ugliness and foreignness
- the **denial of love** sets **aggression** in motion: society seems responsible for the existence of evil, Monster only turns bad because of unjust rejections
- **question of humanity:** the Monster is an artificial creature and is torn between innate humanity and indescribable cruelty; however, Frankenstein could be regarded as the real monster as well: he becomes less and less human and socially integrated during his inhuman endeavour to create life; by shunning responsibility for the Monster, he sets the disastrous events in motion

Hamlet

1 Key facts about the play

- **full title:** *Hamlet – The Tragedy of Hamlet, Prince of Denmark*
- **author:** William Shakespeare (1564–1616)
- **year of writing:** around 1601
- **year of publication:** 1602: entry was made in the Stationers' Register; 1603 (First Quarto); 1604 (Second Quarto); 1623 (First Folio)
- **genre:** tragedy, revenge drama
- **structure:** five acts
- **language:** about two-thirds in **blank verse** (traditional in Elizabethan dramas), i.e. lines do not rhyme, metre: iambic pentameter (five feet to each line, each foot contains two beats, with the stress on the second beat); one-third in **prose:** as the protagonist Hamlet speaks more than one third of the play's lines, this rather large proportion of prose is indicative of his inner conflicts and insecurity about himself, because he mainly uses prose in scenes of "madness" or heightened emotional tension
- **setting:** Denmark, Danish court, Elsinore Castle; time undefined (late Middle Ages)
- **content:** The old King Hamlet of Denmark died suddenly. After his death, his brother Claudius hastily marries King Hamlet's widow, Gertrude, and takes the throne for himself. Gertrude's son Hamlet, the Prince of Denmark, learns from his father's Ghost that Claudius has killed him. The Ghost commands Hamlet to exact revenge for the murder. Hamlet is set on carrying out this demand but delays it for different reasons. The tragedy ends with the death of almost all the main characters.

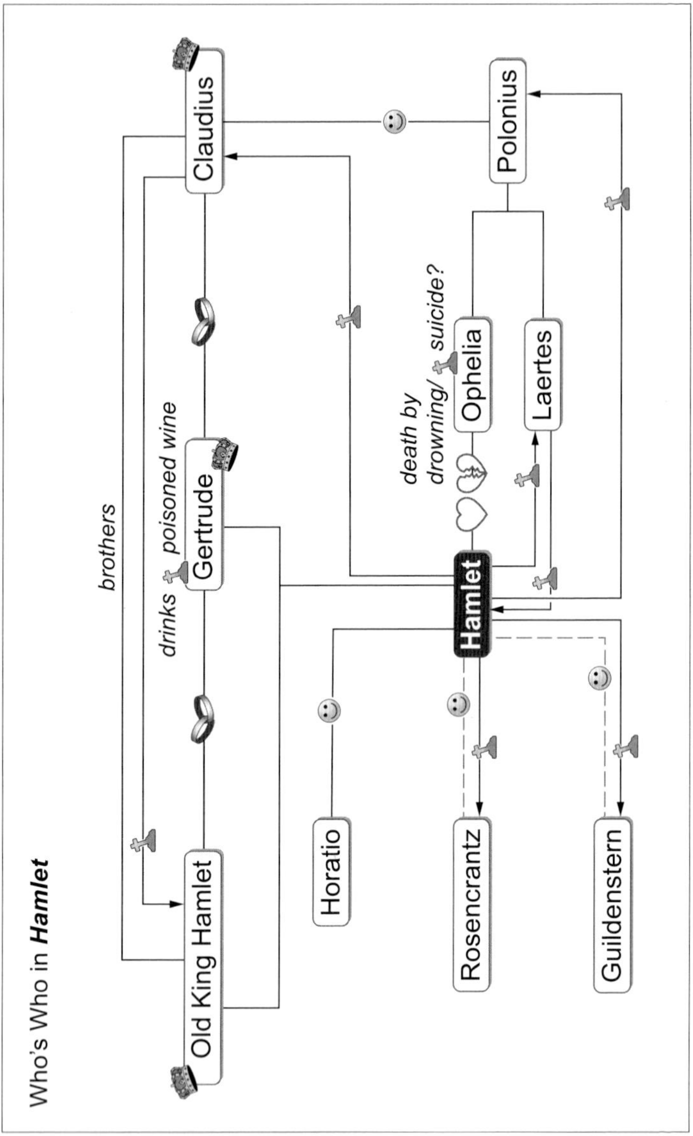
Who's Who in *Hamlet*
Old King Hamlet
Gertrude
Claudius
brothers
drinks poisoned wine
Polonius
Ophelia
death by drowning/ suicide?
Laertes
Hamlet
Horatio
Rosencrantz
Guildenstern

2 Plot[2]

Act I

Act I, Scene 1 | **a platform upon the fortifications of the castle**

- The guardsmen Marcellus and Bernardo ask Horatio, a Danish gentleman, to watch out with them for the Ghost of the recently deceased King Hamlet of Denmark, which has appeared to them before.
- Horatio is at first sceptical, but when the Ghost reappears, he recognises the battle armour the king had worn in a fight with Fortinbras, King of Norway.
- Horatio is worried that the Ghost might have been sent as a warning of an imminent attack by young Fortinbras of Norway. As it does not speak to them, he decides to inform Prince Hamlet, the old King's son and his closest friend.

Act I, Scene 2 | **the hall of the castle**

- King Claudius, the former king's brother, professes to mourn the old king's death, but at the same time, he is happy about his marriage to Gertrude, the old king's widow and Hamlet's mother.
- Claudius sends two of his courtiers, Cornelius and Voltimand, to Norway. They are supposed to ask the ageing king Fortinbras to stop his nephew, young Fortinbras, from trying to take control over Denmark.
- Laertes, the son of Polonius, the king's Lord Chamberlain, is granted permission to return to France, from where he has come to attend the coronation of Claudius.
- Claudius wants his nephew Hamlet to stay in Denmark and not to return to university in Wittenberg. Both he and Gertrude tell Hamlet to stop grieving over his father's death.
- While Hamlet seemingly obeys, he reveals his grief about his father's death and the anger about his mother's remarriage in a monologue.

2 The structure of the play is based on the Reclam edition (1993, edited by Holger Klein).

- He is interrupted by Horatio, Marcellus and Bernardo who tell him about the Ghost. Hamlet agrees to come with them and watch out for it at night.

Act I, Scene 3 **a room in Polonius' quarters**

- Laertes is on the verge of leaving for France: He warns his sister, Ophelia, not to give in to Hamlet's advances but stay away from him. He muses that due to his status as heir to the throne, Hamlet ranks socially much higher than Ophelia and is therefore unlikely to be true to her.
- Polonius, the siblings' father, gives his son some pompous parting advice and repeats Laertes' warnings about Hamlet to Ophelia.
- Ophelia promises to obey her father.

Act I, Scene 4 **the platform upon the fortifications**

- Hamlet meets Horatio and Marcellus on the battlements of the castle to wait for the Ghost to appear.
- They hear Claudius and his men feasting in the castle below, of which Hamlet disapproves.
- The Ghost approaches and motions for Hamlet to leave with it alone.
- Despite the others' warnings, Hamlet follows the Ghost.

Act I, Scene 5 **a more remote part of the fortifications**

- The Ghost confirms that it is Old Hamlet's spirit and that the old king was murdered by his brother Claudius, who poured poison in his ear.
- The Ghost commands Hamlet to seek revenge on his uncle but spare his mother Gertrude.
- When the apparition vanishes, Hamlet asks Horatio and Marcellus to keep quiet about what they have just seen and also about his own plan to feign madness to prove his uncle's guilt.

Act II

Act II, Scene 1 **a room in Polonius' quarters**

- Polonius gives his servant Reynaldo notes and money to take to Laertes in Paris and instructs him to spy on his son.

- Ophelia, shocked and confused, tells her father about an odd encounter with Hamlet. She believes he has gone mad.
- Polonius suspects Hamlet's madness is the result of lovesickness after Ophelia has rejected him and intends to inform Claudius about it.

Act II, Scene 2 | **the audience chamber, giving on to the lobby**

- Rosencrantz and Guildenstern, two of Hamlet's student friends from Wittenberg, arrive and are greeted by Claudius and Gertrude, who have sent for them because they want them to find out the cause for Hamlet's recently moody behaviour.
- Voltemand and Cornelius report that the king of Norway has stopped young Fortinbras from attacking Denmark. He now plans to attack Poland and asks for permission to pass through Denmark.
- Polonius tells Claudius that Hamlet's "transformation" is due to his unrequited love for Ophelia. They plan to spy on a meeting of the two young lovers to test this theory.
- Polonius speaks to Hamlet, who once more feigns madness. However, as Polonius remarks, "Though this be madness, yet there is method in't."
- Hamlet greets Rosencrantz and Guildenstern and they tell him that they have arranged for an acting company to come and cheer Hamlet up.
- After the actors have arrived, Hamlet asks them to prepare a performance of the play *The Murder of Gonzago* for the following evening.
- In another monologue, Hamlet bemoans his inability to take action and seek revenge for his father. He hopes to find definitive proof of whether his uncle really is guilty of murder from his reaction to the play.

Act III

Act III, Scene 1 | **the audience chamber; later the lobby**

- Rosencrantz and Guildenstern tell Claudius they have tried in vain to find the root of Hamlet's madness.
- Claudius and Polonius hide secretly to overhear a conversation between Hamlet and Ophelia.

- Hamlet enters and delivers his famous soliloquy ("To be or not to be") on suicide, mortality and the human condition.
- When Ophelia arrives, Hamlet behaves increasingly hostile towards her.
- Convinced that Hamlet has become a danger, Claudius decides to send his nephew to England.

Act III, Scene 2 — the hall of the castle

- Before the performance of the play, Hamlet asks Horatio to watch closely for Claudius' reaction.
- When the murder scene of the play is performed, Claudius gets up from his seat and stops the play.
- Hamlet is determined to seek revenge for his father's death after Claudius' reaction apparently betrayed his guilt.
- Rosencrantz, Guildenstern and Polonius ask Hamlet to speak with his mother, who is worried about his recent behaviour.

Act III, Scene 3 — the King's closet

- Claudius fears Hamlet's presence and arranges for him to be sent to England with Rosencrantz and Guildenstern as soon as possible.
- Polonius tells Claudius that Hamlet is on his way to his mother and that he himself plans to hide behind a tapestry and listen in on their conversation.
- When Claudius is alone again, he confesses his crime in prayer and asks for forgiveness.
- Hamlet comes in, but cannot bring himself to carry out the revenge while his uncle is praying.

Act III, Scene 4 — the Queen's closet

- With Queen Gertrude's consent, Polonius hides in her private chambers behind a tapestry to overhear her conversation with Hamlet.
- Hamlet challenges his mother about her relationship with Claudius and flies into an angry rage.
- Fearing for her life, Gertrude cries for help, which makes Polonius react. Hamlet hears the noise and, believing that Claudius is eavesdropping, draws a sword and stabs Polonius.
- Hamlet is rather unperturbed and continues insulting his mother.

- The Ghost appears, reminding Hamlet to seek revenge, but without making his mother suffer. Gertrude cannot see the Ghost.
- Hamlet leaves, dragging the dead body of Polonius from Gertrude's chamber.

Act IV

Act IV, Scene 1 | **the Queen's closet**

- Claudius learns from Gertrude that Hamlet has gone completely mad and killed Polonius.
- Rosencrantz and Guildenstern are to take Polonius' body to the chapel and to leave with Hamlet for England.

Act IV, Scene 2 | **another room in the castle**

- Rosencrantz and Guildenstern find Hamlet, who accuses them of being on Claudius' side and does not want to reveal where Polonius' body is.

Act IV, Scene 3 | **the hall of the castle**

- Hamlet is taken to Claudius under guard, from where he is sent on to England immediately.
- Claudius gives sealed letters for the king of England to Rosencrantz and Guildenstern. In these, he asks for Hamlet's execution.

Act IV, Scene 4 | **the Danish coast near the castle**

- Young Fortinbras leads his troops through Danish territory on their way to Poland.
- On their way to the ship bound for England, Hamlet and his companions meet Fortinbras' captain. Considering Fortinbras' energy in a rather insignificant battle, Hamlet laments his own indecision and inability to act and take revenge for his father's death.

Act IV, Scene 5 | **the Queen's closet**

- The grief over the loss of her father has driven Ophelia mad.
- Laertes returns, determined to avenge his father's death.
- Claudius professes his innocence and offers his help to exact revenge.

Act IV, Scene 6 | **another room in the castle**

- Horatio receives a letter from Hamlet, who has returned to Denmark after pirates attacked the ship bound for England.

Act IV, Scene 7 | **the king's closet**

- Claudius tells Laertes that it was Hamlet who killed Polonius.
- When they learn of Hamlet's return to Denmark, Claudius and Laertes plot his death at a fencing duel between Laertes and Hamlet: Laertes decides to fight with a sharpened sword and to poison the tip of his blade. Should Hamlet be victorious, Claudius prepares a poisoned drink for him.
- Gertrude announces that Ophelia has drowned in a nearby brook.

Act V

Act V, Scene 1 | **a churchyard**

- Two gravediggers dig Ophelia's grave and debate about whether she should receive a Christian burial although her death looks like suicide.
- Hamlet and Horatio arrive and holding a skull in his hands, Hamlet delivers a soliloquy on human mortality.
- During Ophelia's burial service, Hamlet and Laertes fight over her grave.

Act V, Scene 2 | **the hall in the castle**

- Hamlet tells Horatio that he has exchanged the letter for the king of England, which demanded his death, with death orders for Rosencrantz and Guildenstern instead.
- Osric announces that Claudius has bet on Hamlet in a fencing match against Laertes.
- Despite Horatio's warnings, Hamlet accepts the challenge.
- At the fight, Gertrude unwittingly drinks the poisoned wine meant for Hamlet, and dies.
- Laertes manages to wound Hamlet slightly with the poisoned tip of his sword.
- In the heat of the fight, the swords are exchanged and Laertes is wounded by Hamlet with the poisoned weapon.

- Before dying, Laertes admits to plotting against Hamlet and casts blame upon the king. He and Hamlet forgive each other.
- The fatally wounded Hamlet stabs King Claudius and forces him to drink the poisoned wine.
- Hamlet says that young Fortinbras should be the next king of Denmark and dies in Horatio's arms.
- Fortinbras arrives with ambassadors from England, who announce that Rosencrantz and Guildenstern are dead.
- Horatio, the only one alive, receives them and their news.
- Fortinbras laments Hamlet's death and orders his men to give him a soldier's burial.

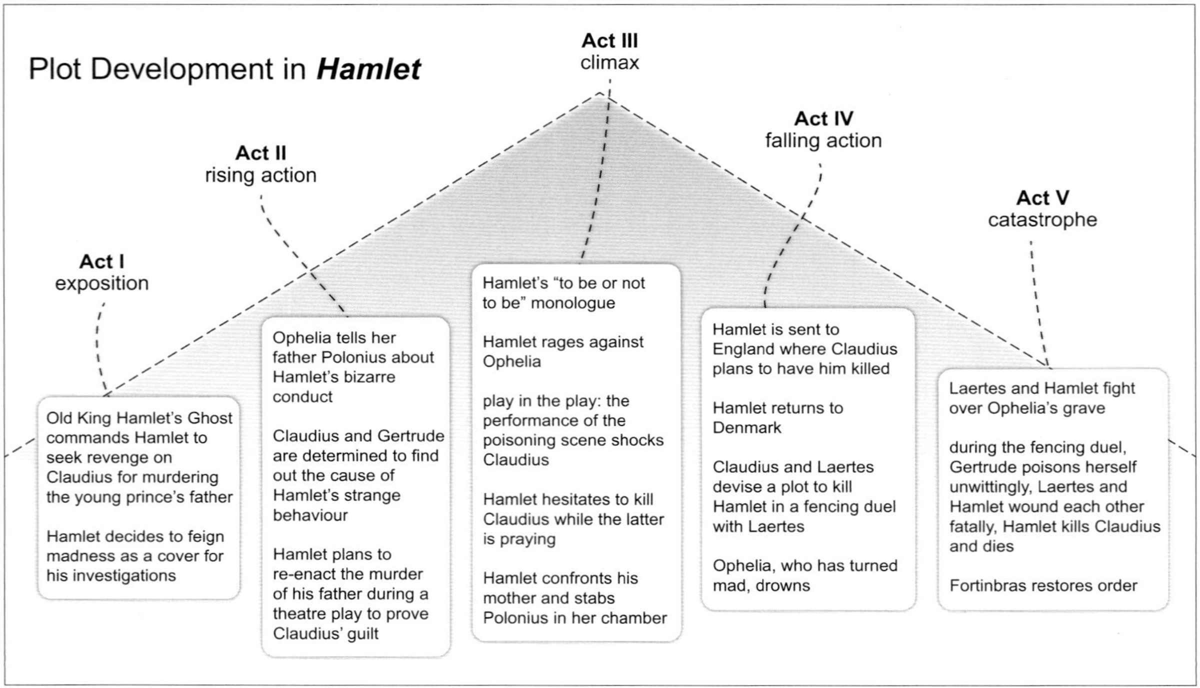
Plot Development in Hamlet
Act I
exposition
Act II
rising action
Act III
climax
Act IV
falling action
Act V
catastrophe
Old King Hamlet's Ghost commands Hamlet to seek revenge on Claudius for murdering the young prince's father
Hamlet decides to feign madness as a cover for his investigations
Ophelia tells her father Polonius about Hamlet's bizarre conduct
Claudius and Gertrude are determined to find out the cause of Hamlet's strange behaviour
Hamlet plans to re-enact the murder of his father during a theatre play to prove Claudius' guilt
Hamlet's "to be or not to be" monologue
Hamlet rages against Ophelia
play in the play: the performance of the poisoning scene shocks Claudius
Hamlet hesitates to kill Claudius while the latter is praying
Hamlet confronts his mother and stabs Polonius in her chamber
Hamlet is sent to England where Claudius plans to have him killed
Hamlet returns to Denmark
Claudius and Laertes devise a plot to kill Hamlet in a fencing duel with Laertes
Ophelia, who has turned mad, drowns
Laertes and Hamlet fight over Ophelia's grave
during the fencing duel, Gertrude poisons herself unwittingly, Laertes and Hamlet wound each other fatally, Hamlet kills Claudius and dies
Fortinbras restores order

3 Characters

Hamlet

- **Prince of Denmark**, son of the late King Hamlet and Queen Gertrude, nephew and stepson of Claudius, very **popular** with the Danish people
- close **friend** of Horatio, also acquainted with Rosencrantz and Guildenstern, **in love** with Ophelia (but later rejects her)
- university **student** in Wittenberg
- **skilful**, **intelligent** and **witty** (plays with words, sees through Claudius' schemes, very philosophical monologues)
- deeply **grieving** his father's death, **enraged** by his mother's remarriage to his uncle
- feels he has to **avenge** his father's murder and kill his uncle, but is very **reluctant** about it
- **sensitive, melancholic, indecisive and brooding** (also aware of his reluctance, envies Fortinbras for his decisiveness, feels bad for not fulfilling his father's wish for revenge, even contemplates suicide)
- on the other hand, also **impulsive** (murder of Polonius, fight with Laertes), **cruel** (towards Gertrude and Ophelia) and **ruthless** (cunningly plotting the murders of Rosencrantz and Guildenstern)
- **madness** real or feigned?
- all in all, a very **ambivalent** character

Claudius

- **Hamlet's uncle and stepfather**, succeeds his brother, Old Hamlet, to the throne and as **Gertrude's husband**
- not entirely clear whether he is really in love with Gertrude or just married her for strategic reasons
- **self-serving, ambitious, ruthless:** murders his brother to assume the throne, his main interest is preserving his power
- **cunning, deceitful, manipulative:** uses poison instead of the sword, uses others to achieve his aims (English king to execute Hamlet, Laertes to kill Hamlet)

Polonius

- Lord Chamberlain, **advisor to King Claudius**
- father of Ophelia and Laertes, **deeply beloved** by his children (Ophelia's madness and Laertes' rage after his death)
- yet, **authoritarian** and somehow **ruthless father** (especially towards Ophelia): demands her obedience, abuses her as bait to get behind Hamlet's madness
- **inquisitive, prying, scheming:** initiates surveillance on Laertes and Hamlet; **eavesdropping** finally costs him his life
- **hypocritical, self-righteous and talkative:** offers wise moral precepts to his son, while thinking nothing of having him spied on; delivers several lengthy, long-winded and boring monologues (despite declaring that "brevity is the soul of wit") (**comical** character)

Laertes

- **Polonius'** son, **Ophelia's** brother
- lives mostly in **Paris**
- apparently close-knit family relationship with Polonius and Ophelia: **strong reaction** to their deaths
- yet, also **patronising** towards his sister and "**mistrusted**" in his **moral behaviour** by his father
- **contrast to Hamlet:** active, sometimes overzealous
- **passionate, easily manipulated and drawn to revenge:** dies from his own sword and scheme

Gertrude

- **Queen of Denmark**, Old King Hamlet's **widow**, married to her brother-in-law Claudius, Hamlet's **mother**
- difficult to judge: either **naive and dependent** on powerful men in her life or **cunning and interested in self-preservation** and her status in society
- not clear whether she knows of (or even had a part in) Claudius murdering her husband (possibly guilty of **adultery**?)
- Old Hamlet's Ghost begs Hamlet to **spare Gertrude**

- **Hamlet despises her** for her marriage to Claudius, **yet** he **seems to love her deeply** (her death, indirectly from Claudius' hands, finally pushes him to killing his uncle)

Ophelia

- **Polonius'** daughter, **Laertes'** sister
- **patronised** by her father and brother
- **romantic relationship** with Hamlet (intensity and seriousness on Hamlet's part unclear)
- **innocent victim:** unjustly insulted by Hamlet, used as a pawn by Claudius and her father Polonius
- after her father's death and Hamlet's rejection: **loses her sanity** and drowns (potentially **suicide**)

Horatio

- Hamlet's **close friend**
- scholar at Wittenberg university
- **loyal and reliable:** supportive of Hamlet, even wants to die with him
- probably the **most "stable" and rational character:** when he sees the Ghost, despite his initial scepticism, this can be seen as evidence of the Ghost being real; is the only one to stay alive to tell the tragic story and transfer the power to Fortinbras

Minor characters

- **Ghost of Hamlet's father:** apparently not only a figment of Hamlet's imagination, because it can also be seen by other characters (though not heard and not by Gertrude in III, 4); sets the action in motion by revealing Old Hamlet's murder and commanding revenge
- **Rosencrantz and Guildenstern:** Hamlet's old friends from Wittenberg; pawns in Claudius' and Hamlet's game
- **Fortinbras:** Prince of Norway, nephew to the old Norwegian king of the same name; contrast to Hamlet: determined, strong and valiant
- **Marcellus, Bernardo and Francisco:** guardsmen at Elsinore

- **Voltemand, Cornelius and Osric:** courtiers
- **Reynaldo:** Polonius' servant
- **a company of players:** sent for to cheer Hamlet up; perform the play in the play *The Murder of Gonzago* by which Claudius' guilt becomes apparent to Hamlet
- **two clowns/gravediggers**

4 Themes and interpretation

Fate vs. free will

The Renaissance was a time in which different world views coexisted. On the one hand, the view of the individual who can shape his or her destiny was beginning to take hold. At the same time, a lot of people believed that their lives were predetermined by fate or divine Providence. In *Hamlet* elements of both concepts can be found.

Background information

free will	– **Machiavellian political philosophy** stressed the notion of free will and an individual who is in full control of his or her life. – In *Hamlet*, there is a **strong juxtaposition of active characters** (e. g. Fortinbras, Laertes) **and the passive**, hesitating and insecure Hamlet.
fatalism	– At the same time, the ancient idea of a "**wheel of fortune**" was still very much alive. It said that Goddess Fortune (Fate) turns her wheel, bringing people from the bottom to the top and letting those at the top fall down again. In other words, those who **rise** to power will inevitably lose their power again and **fall**. – In Christian terms, there was the widespread belief that everything happens according to some greater, **divine plan** and that sinners will ultimately be punished for their deeds (**divine justice**). – In *Hamlet*, the reason for Denmark being a state in which "something is rotten" is the illegitimate assumption of the throne by Claudius. This act has **corrupted the whole political order**. So, in a way, the coming tragedy seems **inevitable**. Order can only be restored with the destruction of the former royal family and the reform of the state by Fortinbras.

Fate and free will in *Hamlet*

- The **Ghost** and its demands (Act I) personify **fate** because it shows Hamlet the course of action he *has to* follow. (Hamlet in I, 4: "My fate cries out", meaning it is his destiny to follow the Ghost)
- However, while Hamlet is on the one hand almost "forced" to follow the Ghost's orders, he is at the same time very **reluctant** to do so. (He realises his inability to cope with the enormous task and curses it, "The time is out of joint. O cursed spite/That ever I was born to set it right!", I, 5)

- In that, *Hamlet* is **different from "normal" revenge tragedies** because it focuses so much on the **inner motivations** of its protagonist and the morality of taking revenge. Hamlet's hesitations, doubts and moral insecurities make him a very **modern hero** because he knows that it is up to him to decide and act, which he continuously delays.
- In his **famous soliloquy** ("To be, or not to be?", III, 1), Hamlet wonders whether it is nobler to suffer through all the terrible things fate throws at people or to fight off the troubles and end them through suicide.
- In the end, the **deaths in V, 2** are provoked by Hamlet's one rash action against Polonius. Still, Laertes acquits Hamlet of his responsibility and gives the catastrophe an **ill-fated** guise when he says: "Exchange forgiveness with me, noble Hamlet,/Mine and my father's death come not upon thee,/Nor thine on me." (V, 2)
- In summary, Hamlet does not present the audience so much with a contrast between fate and free will, but rather **the issue of free will** and having to decide **is problematised:** Hamlet knows what he is supposed to do, namely to kill his uncle Claudius. Yet, he continuously contemplates ways to circumvent, rather than fulfil his fate. In the end, he does fulfil the Ghost's revenge mission, but to his own detriment.

Hamlet's problems with free will

starting point	Hamlet swears to his father's Ghost that he will follow its orders and kill Claudius (I, 5).
indecision	While he feigns to be mad, Hamlet expounds on the very real problem of not being able to decide what is good or bad, true or untrue ("for there is nothing either good or bad, but thinking makes it so.", II, 2).
self-doubt	Hamlet is disgusted with himself because comparing his own reasons for revenge with the player's emotional depth at performing a merely fictional scene, his reaction seems unsatisfactory ("Am I a coward?", II, 2).
insecurity/ uncertainty	Hamlet justifies his hesitation to act with needing absolute proof of his uncle's guilt: he is not sure about the Ghost's honesty and intentions ("The spirit that I have seen/May be a devil", II, 2). So, he plans to re-enact the murder of his father during the production of *The Murder of Gonzago* to gain certainty ("the play's the thing/Wherein I'll catch the conscience of the King.", II, 2).

reflections on suicide/thoughts of escape	Hamlet's melancholy deepens; he reflects on the futility of life and contemplates suicide ("To be, or not to be, that is the question", III, 1). Once more, uncertainty stops him ("But that the dread of something after death –/The Undiscovered country, from whose bourn/No traveller ever returns – puzzles the will,/And makes us rather bear those ills we have/Than fly to others that we know not of?", III, 1).
wrong timing	After the play in the play, Hamlet has seemingly enough reason to finally slay Claudius. Yet, he finds his uncle in his chamber in prayer and forgoes the opportunity to kill him, justifying his hesitation with not wanting the repentant king to go to heaven (III, 3).
weakness	Hamlet admires Fortinbras' fighting spirit and, comparing it to his own "dull revenge", feels shame (IV, 4).
resignation	The final fight comes about because Hamlet does not care about his future any longer (and is resigned to his fate) ("thou wouldst not think how ill all's here about my heart – but it is no matter. [...] If it be now, 'tis not to come; if it be not to come, it will be now; if it be not now, yet it will come – the readiness is all.", V, 2).

The role(s) of women

During Shakespeare's time, women were **socially and financially dependent** on men and expected to obey their husbands (one of the most prominent exceptions being the "Virgin Queen" Elizabeth I, who was unmarried and ruled the country for over 40 years). In the Elizabethan theatre, women were not allowed on stage, so the female characters had to be played by boy actors.

In *Hamlet*, the only female characters are **Ophelia** and **Gertrude**. Both women are manipulated by the **egoistic, authoritarian male characters**. Both eventually die a **tragic death**.

As so often in Shakespeare's works, it remains **open to debate** whether the apparent **misogyny** and suppression of women is simply an expression of prevailing attitudes of the time or whether the Bard indirectly criticises the treatment of women as **inferior and disrespected tools in a man's world**.

Gertrude's depiction in the play

background:

- Queen of Denmark, widow of Old Hamlet, now married to Claudius
- motivation for marriage unclear: her dependency on men?; eager to maintain her social standing?; seduced/persuaded by Claudius?; in love with Claudius?
- heavily criticised by her son Hamlet
- tragic death: unwittingly drinks poisoned wine

two possible interpretations of Gertrude's character:

- She was in an adulterous relationship with Claudius before Old Hamlet's death. She married him only months after losing her first husband because she is **power-hungry and immoral**.
- She is **helpless, naive and dependent** on men to give her security. She is truly unaware of having married a murderer.

men's reactions:

- **Claudius:** Gertrude helps him to keep Denmark stable in difficult times, e. g. during the impending conflict with Norway ("Our queen/ Th'imperial jointress to this warlike state", I, 2), and she was one reason why he killed Old Hamlet ("since I am still possessed/ Of those effects for which I did the murder: / My crown, mine own ambition, and my queen", III, 3). Yet, when Gertrude tells him about Hamlet's rage in her chamber and his killing of Polonius, his only reaction is to fear for his own security ("It had been so with us had we been there.", IV, 1). → It remains unclear whether there is **true love** between Claudius and Gertrude **or** whether one or both of them are **only interested in the other's utility for their schemes**.

- **the Ghost:** It calls her a "most seeming-virtuous queen" and thinks she was seduced by "that incestuous, that adulterate beast" (I, 5). Twice, it asks Hamlet to spare his mother ("Taint not thy mind, nor let thy soul contrive/ Against thy mother aught, leave her to heaven,/ And to those thorns that in her bosom lodge/To prick and sting her.", I, 5; "But look, amazement on thy mother sits./ O, step between her and her fighting soul., III, 4). → For the Ghost, Gertrude is the **less**

guilty party of the adultery. Still, it thinks she has reasons to be **troubled by her conscience**.

- **Hamlet:** Hamlet's **misogyny** is triggered by his mother's marriage to Claudius ("frailty, thy name is woman!", I, 2). There are different interpretations as to why he reacts so strongly to it: Hamlet is obsessed with female sexuality and **advocates a certain ideal of women's "purity"** to which his mother does not live up, or he feels he has to take **his dead father's role** and must act jealous on his part.

Ophelia's depiction in the play

background:

- Polonius' daughter, Laertes' sister, in love with Hamlet (despite being his social inferior)
- becomes the unsuspecting **victim in the web of intrigues** and deceits spun at the Danish court
- the stress becomes so unbearable that she eventually **breaks down and loses her sanity**
- in contrast to Gertrude's, Ophelia's innocence is indisputable

Ophelia as an innocent victim of men's machinations:

- Her father **Polonius** shows **no respect for Ophelia's feelings:** At first, he is very keen to **protect her (and his own) "honour"**, patronisingly tells her to end her relationship with Hamlet and belittles her own judgement of his affection ("Marry, I will teach you: think yourself a baby,/That you have ta'en these tenders for true pay,/ Which are not true sterling; tender yourself more dearly,/Or (not to crack the wind of the poor phrase,/Running it thus) you'll tender me a fool.", I, 3). Later on, he and Claudius have **no scruples to use her** in their plan to find out the reasons for Hamlet's madness.
- Her **relationship with Hamlet** becomes more and more **strained:** She is one of the first to be "affrighted" by Hamlet's madness (II, 2), she has to reject him on her father's orders ("as you did command,/I did repel his letters, and denied/His access to me.", II, 2) and then is **cruelly and unjustly insulted** by Hamlet, who transfers

his disgust with his mother on women in general ("Get thee to a nunnery; why wouldst thou be a breeder of sinners?", III, 1).

- Despite his rejection of her, Hamlet still makes **jokes with sexual innuendo** towards Ophelia ("Lady, shall I lie in your lap?"/"No, my lord."/"I mean, my head upon your lap?"/"Ay, my lord."/"Do you think I meant country matters?"/"I think nothing, my lord."/ "That's a fair thought to lie between maids' legs.", III, 2). It is never revealed whether Hamlet and Ophelia did have a **sexual relationship**, but if yes, Ophelia's madness is also understandable from being a "fallen woman" deserted by her lover.
- Ophelia's **madness** seems to be mainly **caused by Polonius' death**, which leaves her completely **without male protection**.
- The **songs** that mad Ophelia sings also point to another interpretation: They are characteristic for a **woman torn between the strict expectations of her gender and her passionate, but rejected first love** ("Quoth she, Before you tumbled me,/You promised me to wed. […]/So would I 'a' done, by yonder sun,/An thou hadst not come to my bed.", IV, 5).
- Ophelia's death, which is possibly **suicide**, can be seen as the only way for her to take her fate into her own hands and **escape** her oppressive reality. Only in death is she praised again by Hamlet ("I loved Ophelia, forty thousand brothers/Could not with all their quantity of love/Make up my sum.", V, 1) and Laertes, for whom her innocence and purity are still paramount ("Lay her i'th' earth,/ And from her fair and unpolluted flesh/May violets spring", V, 1).

Questions of morality

By definition, the term morality means **the setting of standards or principles of good and bad behaviour**, the distinction between what is right and wrong. Shakespeare's contemporaries were familiar with the **morality plays**. These were plays in which personified virtues and vices tempted the human protagonist to engage in good or evil deeds. After his fall, the protagonist was redeemed and the order restored.

In *Hamlet*, at a superficial glance, there also seems to be a **development** from "the rotten state of Denmark" (cf. I, 4), which has come about through Claudius' unnatural and clearly evil act of murdering his brother, to the restoration of order through Fortinbras. Yet, especially the protagonist Hamlet – and to a lesser extent, some other main characters, too – cannot unambiguously be **judged as moral or immoral**.

The good-evil continuum in ***Hamlet***

Morality is one of the main themes of the play and also preoccupies Hamlet himself. He feels he is in a desperate situation where **both action** (taking revenge, respectively killing himself) **and inaction** (leaving things as they are) can be seen as **morally wrong**.

quotes from the play

- "To be, or not to be, that is the question –/Whether 'tis nobler in the mind to suffer/The slings and arrows of outrageous fortune,/Or to take arms against a sea of troubles/And, by opposing, end them." (III, 1)
- "I must be cruel only to be kind;/Thus bad begins, and worse remains behind." (III, 4)

Hamlet torn between good and evil

Hamlet as a good character	Hamlet as an evil character
Hamlet is honest and sensitive. He genuinely suffers from his father's death.	His feigned madness is a cover for his irresolution and cruel actions, e. g. towards Ophelia and Gertrude.
He is morally justified in his rage against his father's murderer.	He kills Polonius in a rage.
He is loved and respected by his friends (esp. Horatio) and also by the Danish people.	He has Rosencrantz and Guildenstern ruthlessly murdered even though they were probably unknowing pawns in Claudius' scheme.
It is indicative of Hamlet's morality that he does not rush into violence easily, but has moral doubts.	He does carry his revenge through on Claudius, but is also (in)directly responsible for the deaths of Laertes, Gertrude and Ophelia.
Through the **many monologues** that allow the audience an **inward view of Hamlet's mind** (and maybe exactly because of his **moral ambivalence**), he is easy to empathise or even identify with. That is why Hamlet is generally a **very popular literary character**.	